Behavioral Strategies for Classroom Management

John P. Glavin
Temple University

Charles E. Merrill Publishing Company
A Bell & Howell Company
Columbus, Ohio

The Charles E. Merrill Series on
Behavioral Techniques in the Classroom

Thomas M. Stephens, consulting editor

Published by
Charles E. Merrill Publishing Company
A Bell & Howell Company
Columbus, Ohio 43216

Copyright © 1974 by Bell & Howell Company. All rights reserved. No part of this book may be reproduced in any form, electric or mechanical, including photocopy, recording, or any information storage and retrieval system, without permission in writing from the publisher.

International Standard Book Number: 0-675-08873-9

Library of Congress Catalog Card Number: 73-86934

Printed in the United States of America

1 2 3 4 5 6 7 8 – 79 78 77 76 75 74

FOREWORD

The Merrill Series on Behavioral Techniques in the Classroom has as its major objective *the improvement of academic and social instruction.* By using textbooks that focus on systematic applications of behavioral technology in school settings, future practitioners will be better equipped to assist students in at least three ways. When applied by trained personnel, behavioral techniques accelerate learning, decelerate undesirable responses, and help maintain learned responses.

Social and academic skills and attitudes are typically acquired more rapidly through behavioral approaches than when instruction occurs in more conventional ways. The specificity of instructional objectives, the analysis of functioning prior to instruction, the careful application of instructional strategies, and the incentives for responding all contribute to rapid learning and efficient teaching.

Maladaptive, inappropriate, and incorrect responses are modified and reduced in frequency of occurrences. A combination of deliberate activities by teachers results in a reduction of undesirable responses. Whenever possible, incorrect behavior is not reinforced. Also, conditions are arranged to reduce the chances of wrong emissions. And as more time is spent in correct responding, less time is available for undesired behavior.

Behavioral approaches can be effective in helping to maintain past learnings. The functional ways in which learning occurs encourage the use of such learning which contributes to maintenance of responses. Although behavior maintenance has not been demonstrated as well as initial learning through behavioral approaches, the focus on observable responses seemingly facilitates learning and performance across time intervals.

Each text in this series is devoted to a particular aspect of schooling and/or behavioral methodology. This text focuses on modifying disruptive behavior in the regular classroom. However, the author places management of conduct behavior in its proper perspective; within the context of classroom instruction and academic learning, he describes how teachers can effectively prevent as well as correct student behavior problems.

This book deals with the current issues which accompany the use of behavior modification techniques in schools. You will also be informed about the various aspects of behavioral approaches: what each is, how it is applied, when it should be used, and how it should be evaluated.

You will not learn all there is to know about behavior modification on these pages. No one book could provide a sufficient amount of information to achieve that goal. However, the contents of this book should be more than adequate for anyone who wishes to implement behavioral approaches in a classroom. This book can get one started toward the goal of improving instruction. It can encourage readers to apply behavioral techniques, and it will serve as a guide to those who wish to improve their teaching.

Professor Glavin has presented the technology and theory of behavior modification in clear, concise language. Those who read this book can not help but learn from it. This book will get you started, but once it has done that, it will be up to you to implement those practices which are presented here.

Thomas M. Stephens
Consulting Editor

PREFACE

Education today faces many paradoxes. Regular classroom teachers often maintain that classroom management is their most serious problem, while many special educators report that management problems have decreased with their successful application of behavior modification techniques. Special educators, who are most aware of the labeling and segregation policies which effect exceptional children, declare that many mildly and moderately handicapped children should return to the regular classroom. Many regular class teachers argue against this, claiming they have neither the training, time, nor techniques to cope with these children. Special educators respond by suggesting that *all* teachers use the new techniques, including behavior modification, which have been found to be successful in special classes. Regular teachers, driven by conscientiousness—and perhaps desperation—have sought out research literature on behavior modification in the classroom, and more often than not the reaction is "That's well and good. However, in the regular classroom we have one teacher to an average of twenty-five to forty students; in the special classroom there is usually one teacher (often assisted by an aide) to an average of eight or nine students." And it is true that in dealing with special children on a lower teacher-pupil ratio, special education tends toward special methods—methods which the regular classroom teacher cannot embrace very well unless sufficient modifications are made.

One approach which has proven to be exceedingly successful is Behavior Modification. With the use of behavioral techniques comes the need for management, and in turn, the need for manpower. Behavioral analysis utilizes the following basic procedures for changing behavior in children: (1) Selecting a target of behavior; (2) changing the behavior's consequences; (3) keeping records; (4) shaping the behavior; and (5) continuously evaluating the data. In a special class, where the teacher-pupil ratio is one to eight, it is difficult to manage these procedures; special education teachers who work in higher teacher-pupil ratio classrooms find it even more impracticable. Regular classroom teachers, who have teacher-pupil ratios as high as one to thirty-five, would find a typical behavior modification procedure not only impracticable, but irrelevant as well.

Our goal is to find a satisfactory way to facilitate behavior modification not only in the special classroom, but also in the regular classroom, where the current lack of manpower and funds makes the initiation of this kind of program unfeasible. This volume is an attempt to describe a realistic concept which will enable the regular classroom teacher to more clearly see his place in the management of children's problems. The first section critically evaluates the present position of applying behavior modification in various classroom settings. Chapter 1 introduces the reader to current trends in education for handling behavior problem children. The interaction between the child and his classroom environment in creating deviant behavior is stressed in Chapter 2. Behavior modification procedures as they are most commonly applied today, and a critical evaluation of these procedures, are presented in Chapters 3 and 4.

Section 2 of this book discusses different types of reinforcement procedures and teaching strategies which could help make behavior modification more practical for the regular class teacher. The critical question asked of each procedure is whether it is feasible to apply in a regular class setting. In contrast to Section 1, which emphasizes token economies and extrinsic reinforcement, the topics in Section 2 present a hierarchy of procedures and strategies leading ultimately to self-managed and intrinsic reinforcement.

The remainder of the volume (Chapters 10 and 11) is devoted to concomitant topics often felt to be useful or necessary to applying behavior modification in the classroom, but which are seldom emphasized, or even mentioned, in textbooks on the subject. The importance of individualizing instruction, and the various facets of classroom structure are discussed in Chapter 10. The final Chapter stresses the vital role of the regular class teacher in the successful implementation of a behavioral approach to teaching. *Behavioral Strategies for Classroom Management* is accompanied by an appendix which evaluates commercial curriculum materials.

CONTENTS

Section 1 Behavior Modification Practices and Procedures Today

1. The Mergence of Special and Regular Education, 5
2. Managing Classroom Behavior, 18
3. Behavior Modification as Applied Today, 32
4. Some Reflections on Behavior Modification in the Classroom, 44

Section 2 Different Types of Reinforcement Procedures and Teaching Strategies

5. Modeling and Vicarious Reinforcement, 57
6. Social Reinforcement, 67
7. Contingency Contracting: From Teacher to Self-Control, 83
8. Peer Tutoring, 94
9. Self-management in Learning, 106

Section 3 Postscripts to Behavior Modification in the Classroom

10. Individualization and Structure in the Classroom, 117

11   The Teacher Variable, 128

Appendix: Evaluation of Commercial Curriculum Materials, 135

Name Index, 147
Subject Index, 150

Section 1

Behavior Modification Practices and Procedures Today

1

The Mergence Of Special And Regular Education

Special education has traditionally referred to the education of special, i.e., exceptional children. Although every child is in some sense exceptional, technically the exceptional child is one who deviates from the average or normal behavior to such a degree that he needs special attention.

At one time, exceptional individuals were viewed as deviants from whom the remainder of society fled, as though deviance was contagious. This general attitude was noticeably reflected in our educational policies through which we attempted to isolate the "abnormals" from the "normals." This took the form of special classes designed to carry on programs for children who couldn't adjust to the regular class program. However, programs for both regular and exceptional students were uniform for all children in the same grouping. There was little consideration of each child's individuality in either one of the two classroom situations. The mergence of both regular and special education is due to two main trends: the increasing emphasis on personalizing and individualizing all instruction, and on normalizing the exceptional. Both indicate refreshing new social attitudes toward all children, normal and handicapped.

In the past a teacher wrote out a detrimental little form termed a *referral* for a student who had academic difficulty, whose behavior was disruptive to the class, or who was too difficult for her to handle well. Although many are quick to point an accusing finger at the teacher, one must consider that one instructor with thirty-five pupils, perhaps a third of whom are acting out behavior problems, could be in a very frustrating position. This teacher has very little knowledge about each pupil as a unique individual with a different emotional and academic background. Our educational system does not provide the teacher with sufficient information or training to provide remedial help, extra material, or whatever she may need to make each individual's education meaningful. In special classes, the same thing has been allowed to happen, whether it is in the public schools, or in government-sponsored institutions. This is due in part to the attitude that exceptional children, sharing the same "symptons," are suffering from the same "disease."

The most controversial current issue in special education is that of integration versus segregation of the exceptional child. Positions on the integration versus segregation issue range from segregation into special schools devoted entirely to exceptional students with a specific handicap, to complete integration of the students in regular classrooms. Dunn (1968), Christoplos and Renz (1970) are the strongest proponents of abolition of segregated classes for educable mentally retarded (EMR) students on the grounds that such placement may be detrimental rather than beneficial. However, as MacMillan (1971) points out, the research evidence on the efficacy of special versus regular class placement of exceptionals remains largely equivocal and inconclusive. Experts representing all the other disability areas besides EMR have also considered the issue of integration versus segragion. It is generally thought that integration, even with its problems and hazards, is still the most beneficial arrangement.

Special Versus Integrated Classrooms

Although, the current trend is for the integration of exceptional children into the regular classroom, the debate on special versus regular classes has been long and involved. There seems to be some evidence that educable retarded pupils in segregated classes may show significantly better social adjustment while those in integrated classes show better academic progress. Christoplos and Renz argue that in the long run, the isolation factor of special classes is socially detrimental. They claim that the exceptional child learns to adjust to the normal world from frequent interaction and that the normal population can learn from the handicapped. The attitudes of fear and rejection are "concomitants of unfamiliarity." If problems arise in the integrated situation between exceptional and normal individuals, there should be "remedial manipulations of the environment before segregation is considered. . ." (p. 378).

The issue of special versus integrated classrooms has political overtones. Sometimes incorrigibles are labeled either emotionally disturbed or mentally retarded and shipped out of the classroom. As education is one of the few ways our society provides for moving to another social level, the disproportionate number of minority group children in special classes has been a cause of growing concern. Because of inferior education and an accompanying low self-image in some of these classes, special education has been accused of denying upward social mobility to oppressed peoples. If indeed the trend for integration continues, where will that put special education teachers?

Another major current trend is to make more effective use of manpower. Special educators may, in the future, multiply their influence by becoming consultants to classroom teachers. Thus, one special education teacher-consultant can influence the exceptional children in an entire district, rather than in just one school.

These factors indicate the need for change in special education organization and operation. Instead of depending primarily on special classes, emphasis must be placed on the actions of regular classroom teachers supported by consultant and resource teachers, and involving only in unusual cases special classes or other separate instruction. Most exceptional children will spend at least part of their time in the regular class.

MacMillan states that "The real issue is not whether special or regular classes are better for the mildly retarded, but rather—the extent to which a wider range of individual differences can be accomodated in the regular class" (p. 401). The general trend for integrated classes, and thus for including a wider range of academic abilities within the classroom, does pose a difficulty for the teacher. The problem of individualized instruction can only be acknowledged as such (see Chapter 9). Literature on precision teaching and on subgroup performance (Chapters 6, 7, 8, 9) may provide more clues to its solution.

Individualization Of Diagnostic And Remedial Techniques

Individual differences are always emphasized in today's teacher training programs. However, students often graduate and become teachers without ever really understanding the meaning of such differences in the classroom, regular or special. The topic of "exceptional children" to most teachers implies students with such extreme differences that they must be in special classes or in institutions— never those students with whom they themselves will have to work! When, on occasion, a child is so obviously different, the first inclination of most teachers is to say that the child does not belong in his classroom, or perhaps not even in the public schools.

When teachers know more of the facts about individual differences and about children who really are exceptional, better comprehension of the general classroom situation is possible. Everyone acknowledges that there are children who are not extreme enough in their differences to need special classes or to receive other special help. Little has been said of these children with milder deviations who are handled merely as "members of the class group." There is a great need for specific principles and practices to be used in taking care of individual differences as they actually occur in the regular classroom. This knowledge must be added to general teacher training principles and methods.

With an individualized system of learning, standardized intelligence tests will have less meaning than they now have. The overrepresentation of minority group children in EMR classes who have mostly motivational rather than cognitive problems illustrates the irresponsibility of classifying children on the basis of such testing. A more valid method for properly placing children in programs would be to observe the cognitive functioning of a child and to study the way a child learns, his capacities and processes. This method would put an end to providing inadequate educational opportunities on the basis of a numerical score, and would be a better assurance that all children would receive an education that would foster their maximum intellectual growth.

A controversy has arisen over what type of curriculum should be offered to the exceptional child: a society-oriented curriculum which molds him into the person society would like him to be, or a child-centered curriculum which allows him to develop his own goals and interests. Too often the educational needs of children are not met because of the inadequate educational opportunities available to them. If certain children do not fit into the regular school system, they are pushed into special education classes because they are not fitting into or not accepting the curriculum that the system, alias society, wants them to accept.

As a reflection of this shift in emphasis to remediation, diagnosticians have begun to employ more instruments amenable to individualized program planning. Non-language tests, "culture fair" tests, instruments yielding a profile of subscores such as the Illinois Test of Psycholinguistic Abilities, behavioral checklists, and better tests of social maturity have been used to supplement the traditional IQ test in order to get a more complete picture of the child's deficits and assets, thereby aiding remedial planning. There is also increasing emphasis being placed on the diagnostic role of the teacher. Because he is most familiar with a child's performance, the teacher is best able to assess the child informally.

The time has come to cease attempting to discover a new universal teaching method. There are hundreds of ways to teach a child and what is needed is clinical teaching in order to match the child with the method from which he will benefit most. This is the idea behind the "precision teaching" method. Of related importance is the idea of a "Learner-Material Match"—a system for selecting appropriate instructional materials based on the learning abilities of the child or group of children in order to get the most beneficial match.

The success of using programmed instruction as a means of individualizing instruction for exceptionals has been affirmed by several educators. Programming allows each child to progress at his own pace. A similar idea is expressed by those who advocate development of non-graded early childhood units in schools, which would extend until the child was eight or nine, and where the language concepts and reading skills essential to all further learning would be developed before the child could move on to a higher elementary school level. With such units in the integrated classrooms, it would be efficacious to divide the large group into smaller subgroups of children functioning on a similar level of proficiency. In this way more individualization could be achieved even in large classrooms.

Although educational philosophies and theories always seem to loom far ahead of their initiation into practice in the school systems, changes are nonetheless taking place. In all areas of education, there is increasing concern for the individual. Much attention is being given to the effectiveness of programmed instruction, which has the advantage of allowing a child to set his own pace in learning and provides him with immediate feedback on his responses, whether they are correct or incorrect. Presently, reading programs are being used which allow one class to learn together, although several different reading levels are incorporated into one group. We have the technology, but not the finance or government priorities, to design programs tailored to the individual needs of each child.

It is assumed that although classification of children does serve some purpose, educators should place less emphasis on labeling children and more on classifying programs, so that children will be placed in the best educational situation for them. Because exceptional children are children first, and then exceptional, care must be taken to place each child, especially borderline cases, in a satisfying situation where growth and learning will take place. One of the best ways to accomplish this is through individualized instruction.

Present Trends—The Labeling Problem

Probably the greatest fault of special education in recent years has been the incorrect labeling of children for school placement. Hall (1970) found that in some instances more than half of the children in Boston's local special education programs had been misclassified. It appears that while assignment of a child to a special class is often unrelated to the needs of the child, it provides a rather convenient parking place for children who present problems in the regular classroom. General education has been accused of failing to adapt to the needs of these children. Special class placement has been accused of being a means of justifying this failure by saying that the problem is within the child, instead of within the educational system which does not individualize its teaching enough to insure every child's development.

Exceptional children exhibit a wide range of individual differences. Many have other modes of functioning that can be developed to compensate for their specific deficiency. Others are multiply handicapped. Labeling fails to account for this wide range of individual differences because it places children in categories which are too strict. As few children fall into a pure type, labeling a child suggests a uniformity about his makeup which does not exist; therefore, differential diagnosis is essential.

The labeling problem has its roots in a traditional categorical grouping approach based on the medical model, and in the inadequacy of diagnostic instruments that are also based on a medical model. These traditional classifications have been criticized for having a limited relevance to educational decisions. For this reason, the diagnostic emphasis is being shifted from etiology to remediation. The focus of attention can then be on external variables about which educators might be able to do something, rather than on a "defect" residing in the child which sets educators free of responsibility for the child's failure.

Many experts have felt that the major impeding factor for success of exceptionals is the *attitude* of nonexceptionals toward them. Segregation leads to ignorance, intolerance, and stereotyping by normal children which is often carried through the lives of exceptional children. Integration of exceptionals, to promote positive attitudes, would allow normal children to understand the exceptional child as an individual and to assess the limitations of a disability realistically. This would be in keeping with the fact that rather than being stereotypes, exceptionals present a wide variety of traits. Integration would also allow exceptional children to better develop the social skills necessary for adult success, improve their self-image by avoiding stigmatization as "special" or "different," and minimize the danger of self-fulfilling prophesies derived from labeling and segregating.

A basic distinction is usually drawn between the mildly handicapped child and the more seriously handicapped. There are many trainable mentally retarded children as well as totally deaf, blind and seriously emotionally disturbed children who deviate too markedly on too many variables to be placed in the regular classroom. For these children, special classes seem inevitable.

Toward More Efficient Use Of Manpower

About ten to twelve percent of the school age population today needs some form of special education (Mackie, 1965) although only about one-half of the nation's school districts maintain or provide such programs. One proposal for surmounting this manpower deficit has been made by Lilly (1971). He outlines a program of the future whereby all mildly handicapped children will be handled in the regular classroom with the support of special educators. The special educator will assume the role of an instructional specialist who "would work with the teacher in such areas as diagnosis of problems in academic skill areas, specification of both individual and small group study programs, behavior management procedures and group and individual reinforcement patterns." Lilly continues, "The child will never be removed from the classroom because this doesn't help the teacher perform her function in the future. The teacher's behavior must be changed and, thereby, the child's" (p. 746).

Although there are now trends in the direction of replacing special classroom teachers with consultants, these tendencies are far from realized. The problem of finding a new system of funding arises. Schools are often paid for the number of children diagnosed under certain labels. Presumably, medical labels will not assume such a great part in the future in special education, nor will children be "exceptional" all the time. It is conceivable that intervention would be necessary for a child at some times and not at others.

Another obstacle in making more efficient use of manpower comes in moving the powers that be. Jones (1971) thinks that "the solution of these 'human problems' (retraining, skill obsolescence, fear of displacement) may well be the most formidable obstacles to full implementation of instructional technology in the educational enterprise" (p. 317). On a pessimistic note, it must be added that several experts have found the competence of special educators quite lacking (MacMillan), and if present special-class teachers are not effective, it is hard to expect regular teachers to handle exceptionals in their classes. Lilly's "training-based model," which advocates use of the special educator as a "teacher educator" who provides support and training for the regular class teacher, can be a valuable approach only when the efficacy of special educators themselves has been proven. As academians, we prefer to look on the brighter side and insist that a "new breed" of highly effective special educators is on the way.

Trends point to the probability that ultimately, for those exceptionals whose handicaps are not in the severe range, general education will accept the responsibility of teaching all children more effectively in the regular class. However, special education will hardly be put out of business. Separate programs will still be needed for those whose educational goals cannot be feasibly met even in an individualized program in the regular classroom.

A hierarchy of special education programs is needed which emphasizes that children should be moved upward, toward "special" treatment for more severe problems only when necessary, and downward, toward normal environments, as soon as is feasible. The basic idea is that the normal environment should very definitely be preserved whenever possible. Before being placed in a full-time special class, the exceptional child should move through trials in the regular class, the regular class with consultation, supplemental teaching in addition to the regular class, the regular class with the resource room for part of the day, and a part-time special class. Also, as soon as possible the exceptional child should be moved out of the full-time special class down the hierarchy with his ultimate goal being placement in the full-time regular class, where he will work on his own individualized program.

MacMillan maintains that while self-contained special classes may be best for certain children, we should have numerous models as alternatives to this in the regular classroom so that as wide a range of students as possible can be accomodated in the regular class. In his view, we need to retrain teachers for this wider range and to establish a closer tie with research so that teachers can take advantage of the newest techniques and materials proven effective.

Special education would then be a resource for the school and would represent more highly trained and specialized teachers. Too often the schools as they are now structured see special education as the babysitting service where troublemakers can be dropped off. Under the new plans, the regular teacher would be required to learn ways of dealing with the exceptional child, or any child, for that matter. This would require better trained teachers and more inservice programs, as well as an alteration in the ways that education is viewed by many, which are variations on "I had to do it this way, why can't they?"

In view of the new directions special educational thought is taking, there are obviously changes needed in the concept of special education itself. Since every child is a little exceptional (so to speak), ideally every teacher should be a special education teacher, in that her orientation would not be the shotgun, middle- of-the-road approach but rather an individually-oriented approach.

Educational Implications

The problems of the exceptional child can and must be dealt with in the public schools. The ideas that special education classes were formed so as not to disturb traditional classes and to act as a fallout for dropouts of the regular educational system must be eradicated. Modification of the regular teacher and classroom must take place. The desired aim of placing many exceptionals back into the regular classroom must be accompanied by some concrete help for the regular classroom teacher.

There has been a move away from blaming a child's progress or lack of success entirely on his pathology, to examining reasons and situations outside of the child. One reason was mentioned above concerning the inadequate educational opportunities available to exceptional children. Another idea has transferred the emphasis from the special child to a special situation in the school, wherein the teacher needs intervention, counseling and modification. The child's failure to learn becomes the failure of the teacher because of her inability to successfully reach that child. MacMillan warns against allowing the integration versus segregation issue to become a quagmire analogous to the nature versus nurture controversy over intelligence. He emphasizes that special education and self-contained classes do not have to be synonymous, and that the larger and more fruitful issue is the extent to which a wider range of individual differences can be accomodated in the regular classroom.

When a child with a learning problem is placed in a regular class, it is still necessary to make adjustments to meet his individual needs. However, as MacMillan notes, if we cannot determine how to individualize in a setting where there is one teacher for fifteen to eighteen children, as evidenced by the criticism of special class efficacy, how can we be ready to individualize in a setting with thirty or more children for one teacher? Therefore it appears premature to abolish special classes for even the mildly handicapped until advances are made on several fronts, namely: individualizing diagnostic and remedial techniques, increasing regular classroom teachers' effectiveness in individualizing curriculum, and finally, motivating and managing individuals and groups of children. When all of these areas have been developed effectively, special education will be able to realize its ultimate goal, at least in terms of the mildly to moderately handicapped, and to work itself out of business as a social institution by turning over to the general educational mainstream whatever helpful technology it develops, so that these handicapped children can be a part of that mainstream. The new educational outlook of special educators is reflected in the above trends. Another major trend is the increasing acceptance of behavior modification.

Behavior Modification

Behavior modification is concerned with changing or modifying isolated behaviors. At one time, a child was said to be emotionally disturbed or "hyperactive, probably suffering from organic brain damage." Now he is said to "get out of his seat, talk loud, pinch others. . . ." In other words, behavior modification does not speak in terms of a some*thing* but of the some*things*: workable, modifiable behavioral units. It is this change in outlook that has opened the way for systematic enviromental manipulations that influence the learning of children. The behavioral approach makes for better communication with classroom teachers, for the changing of specific behaviors has always been the job of teachers. Behavior modification provides a language and framework making duplication of the results of the natural educator or born teacher possible.

Hewett (1967), who set up a classroom for emotionally disturbed children, writes "Rather than view the emotionally disturbed child as a victim of psychic conflicts (psychodynamic approach), cerebral dysfunction (pathological), or merely academic deficits (pedagogical), this approach (behavior modification) concentrates on bringing the overt behavior of the child into line with standards required for learning" (p. 459). Lilly believes that the "emphasis must change from exceptional children to exceptional situations in the school" (p. 745). With the emphasis on specific behaviors, learning as well as behavior problems are handled more concretely.

The use of behavior modification techniques in education has the advantage of applying to children in every diagnostic category. The principles can work with many types of tasks or behaviors. This universality makes it an extremely valuable technique for all educators. The trend toward integration of exceptionals is partly due to the movement to include all educators in what was formerly an innovative technique in special education classes. In other words, the same methods will be used with EMR, emotionally disturbed, learning disabled, gifted, and normal children. Thus a special class of just learning-disabled would be ludicrous. Many educators agree that this will involve a different type of training for teachers so that they can deal with behavioral phenomena as opposed to single disabilities.

All new approaches to special education break from traditional clinical therapy and practice in one way or another. The most encouraging recent development is agreed upon to be the use of behavior modification. These principles have been recently extended from the individual in a clinic to the special classroom group by means of token reinforcement systems and the "engineered classroom" concept of Hewett. The important difference between the behavioral approach and the traditional ones is simply that behavioral approaches have been shown to be effective and to be implemented by special classroom teachers. More work, however, is needed in modifying behavioral techniques for practical use in the large classroom situation.

Research Projects

The Pennsylvania Conference (1972) on Educational Programs for Exceptional Children was held to demonstrate training models emerging in other parts of the United States which were directed to accomodating handicapped children in regular classroom settings. The following descriptions of behavior-oriented programs indicate future trends in the education of exceptional children:

The Professional Instruction Program at Norfolk State College. The primary purpose of the Professional Instructional Program (PIP) is to train regular classroom teachers to meet the special needs of pupils with learning problems in the regular classroom. The instruction during the academic year focuses on language arts and mathematics, with special attention given to diagnosing and prescribing a program of instruction to meet the needs of pupils with learning problems. The teachers were guided in writing behavior objectives and assessing teacher-pupil interaction in the classroom, thus enhancing the pupils' and teachers' self-concepts. The goals of the general program may be listed as: to continue to develop approaches to the training of pre-service teachers, or to the reeducation of experienced ones so as to enable them to deal more effectively with children with learning problems in the regular classroom; to work with heads of elementary education departments and others concerned in effecting change in both elementary and special training programs; to provide, improve and enrich educational experiences for children with learning problems in the regular classroom by training regular classroom personnel in procedures for individualization of instruction; to aid teachers and administrators in acquiring information about the research process, practices, and functions of the field of special education; and to aid parents in developing the ability to solve family living and social problems which affect the learning process of young children.

The Consulting Teacher Program at the University of Vermont. The Consulting Teacher Program was developed, and is being implemented, as a cooperative venture of the Vermont Department of Education, local school districts, and the University of Vermont Special Education Program, with support from USOE, the Bureau of Education for the Handicapped and the Bureau of Education Personnel Development. It provides special education services to children traditionally labelled as learning disabled, mentally retarded and emotionally disturbed. The Consulting Teacher Program works within regular classrooms in the areas of language, arithmetic and social interaction, through consultation and training of regular classroom teachers, school administrators and the parents of referred children.

There was a variety of topics presented at the training conference, including: The use of a behavioral model for providing special education services within regular classrooms, and data demonstrating the effectiveness of the model; consulting-teacher training procedures, and in-service classroom teacher training procedures; consulting procedures; The measuring and evaluating of classroom teaching learning procedures; and developing minimum objectives for *all* children: a new way of defining eligibility and evaluating special education services.

Programmed Environments for the Developmentally Retarded at the University of Kentucky. This project was designed to develop programmed educational interventions for developmentally retarded children commonly called "trainable" or "severely retarded." Its objectives were to develop a programmed environment model for the preschool education of children assumed to be severely retarded/multiply handicapped; to develop a teacher-tutor model through the dissemination of systematic language instruction; to list national research and curriculum development activities which relate to preschool children assumed to be severely retarded/multiply handicapped, and to the young "trainable" retarded child; and to develop competency-based instructional modules for training/retraining staff for programmed environment preschools for individuals assumed to be severely retarded.

Conclusion

The mergence of the exceptional child from the self-contained special classroom to the regular classroom is growing in acceptance, due to such factors as the questioning of labeling practices and the need for more efficient manpower utilization. This necessitates a major overhaul of the regular class teacher's training and role. Behavior modification techniques may prove of value to the teacher if these techniques themselves can be modified to make them applicable to the large classroom situation.

References

Christoplos, F. and P. Renz. "A critical examinationof special education programs." *Journal of Special Education* (1970), *3*, 371–79.

Dunn, L. M. "Special Education for the mildly retarded: Is much of it justifiable?" *Exceptional Children* (1968), *35*, 5–22.

Hall, E. "Special miseducation. The politics of special education." *Inequality in Education*, Harvard Center for Law and Education, Massachusetts, 1970, 17–22.

Hewett, F. M. "Educational engineering with emotionally disturbed children." *Exceptional Children* (1967), *33*, 459–67.

Jones, R. L. *Problems and issues in the education of exceptional children.* New York: Houghton Mifflin Co., 1971.

Lilly, M. "A training based model for special education." *Exceptional Children* (1971), *37*, 745–49.

Mackie, R. P. "Spotlighting advances in special education." *Exceptional Children* (1965), *32*, 77–81.

MacMillan, D. L. "Special education for the mildly retarded: Servant or savant." *Focus on Exceptional Children* (1971), *2*, (9), 1–11.

Newland, T. E. "Why special education." *The Exceptional Child.* J. F. Magary and J. R. Eichorn., eds. New York: Holt, Rinehart and Winston, 1964.

2

Managing Classroom Behavior

Classroom management continues to be one of the most frequently reported problems among teachers. This difficulty is shared by both beginning teachers and those who are more experienced. Teachers appear to be most concerned with controlling acting out-behaviors and with stimulating motivation. In the past, many children who manifested behavior problems were referred to mental health agencies. However, it is becoming obvious that behavioral techniques must be increasingly utilized in the classroom. By incorporating various behavioral strategies which are described later in this chapter, the teacher can deal with classroom management, as well as individual behavior. It is the purpose of this chapter to aid teachers and consultants in more competently assuming the role of behavioral managers. This review will touch on issues such as the nature of deviant classroom behavior, consulting with teachers, teacher strategies for preventing everyday problems, and techniques for specific behavioral problems.

What is Deviant Classroom Behavior?

Within the last decade, learning theory has come into the foreground of explaining behavior. Behavior problems, according to behaviorists, are not now generally viewed as illness. Instead, they are hypothesized as being the result of one or a combination of the following: (1) learning inappropriate skills, (2) faulty learning of appropriate times for certain behaviors, (3) restricted opportunities to learn at all.

The socialization process teaches most children to make themselves more acceptable in terms of the society in which they must participate. If the child fails to learn these means of enhancing his acceptability, he is frequently labeled a behavior problem by important others in his environment. With this focus comes a trend away from placing the responsibility for "sickness" totally within the pupil. As medical diagnoses and consequent labels become somewhat obsolete, referral to outside treatment agencies becomes less necessary. The child's teacher and school consultant may now take a more active responsibility for producing behavioral change.

By defining deviant behavior as an interaction between the faulty learning of the child and the expectations functioning within his environment, the teacher can understand that classroom deviancy is not always a one-sided affair. As is discussed in the chapters on contingency-management, self-management and peer-tutoring, the classroom need not be a one-sided, sterile learning environment, but rather one which involves an exchange of the curriculum between teachers and students. Teaching and learning transactions are special kinds of interpersonal relationships; the way in which pupils experience the curriculum is influenced not only by their relationships with the teacher, but also through their contact with peers. The teacher is typically singled out as the most influential classroom participant, since he is formally charged with presenting the curriculum and with improving interpersonal relationships, but perhaps his most important duty is deciding the amount of freedom allowed in his classroom. This decision will influence greatly who and how many children are thought to be behaviorally deviant in his classroom.

In the traditional classroom where the teacher makes most or all of the decisions, there tends to be an emphasis on "lock-step" curriculum procedures—rules or a list of "don'ts" and conformity. The "deviants" in this classroom are those children who either cannot measure up to the expected norm or those who will not do as prescribed by the teacher. This classroom teacher inclines towards the use of grading or censuring the child depending upon whether he can or cannot measure up to his peers. When a behavioral modification approach is used in the traditional classroom setting, the likelihood is greater that an extrinsic reinforcement system will be employed.

Once the teacher delegates some of her control and responsibilities to others in the class, the criteria for classroom deviancy shifts. For instance, when peer tutoring is employed, the former series of "don'ts" is replaced by needs on the part of students to talk, to help rather than compete, and to socialize. Consequently, these are the behaviors that are most highly esteemed, whereas not talking, not helping and not interacting are the deviant behaviors.

If the teacher utilizes contingency contracting, students are likely to show a change from group discipline, emphasizing external stimuli and control, to self-discipline, reflecting increased responsibility for sharing and making decisions concerning oneself. Deviant behavior shifts with this system to an inability or unwillingness to accept increased decision-making responsibility. Reinforcement is much more likely to be of an intrinsic nature than it was in previous classroom atmospheres.

The above references to the characteristics of various teaching styles is not made to denigrate the traditional classroom style, but to demonstrate the relativism of what determines deviant classroom behavior. It is not inconceivable that the experienced teacher might wish to employ several or all of the various decision-making approaches at different times of the day.

Consulting with Teachers

The selection of an appropriate intervention for the behavior problem child continues to raise questions and problems. One problem is attaining efficiency in delivering teacher services. Removal to a special class may relieve the regular classroom teacher of a burden. However, the teacher assigned to the small number of children served daily in the special class is usually unable to work with additional children who have a marginal hold in regular class but who are in need of special help. Therefore, the special class plan limits or precludes the delivery of partial service to those children whose problems are of recent origin, specific to certain parts of the school program, or barely tolerable to the regular classroom teacher.

It is projected that ninety percent (Long, Morse and Newman, 1971) of behavior problem children remain in regular classrooms and do not receive adequate special education services. Glavin, Quay, Annesley, and

Werry (1971) increased the delivery potential of the special teacher by establishing resource rooms for some behavior problem children. These children, who received academic instruction in resource rooms for one or two hours daily, showed improvement in both resource room behavior and performance on standardized tests of academic achievement. However, the behavioral improvements did not generalize to the regular classrooms, where the children continued to spend the greater portion of their school day.

These observations and other such factors as the labeling problem and the necessity for developing programs without much additional financial support from the community, prompted a study (Quay, Glavin, Davis, and Mishkin, 1971) using behavior modification procedures with behavior problem children in regular classrooms within a consultative model carried out by in-training behavioral consultants. Each consultant advised two first-year elementary regular classroom teachers who were experiencing difficulty with classroom management. Results of the study illustrated two types of problems that minimally experienced consultants might encounter.

The problems encountered by consultants attempting to involve teachers in programs have received little attention; yet the success of a consulting program depends upon the teacher's adherence to the advice given by the consultant. Our experience has demonstrated that our in-training consultants and the research design both contributed to the lack of success. First of all it would appear to be far more effective to be asked for help than to present program ideas and to request volunteers or assign teachers to carry them out. Yet, to avoid the biases introduced by volunteer teachers, the experimental teachers in this pilot study were randomly selected. Second, while our intervention program started for all experimental teachers at the same time, it is probably wiser to start on a small scale with a few highly motivated teachers, thus improving the likelihood of maximal success. Finally, serveral of our intervention strategies involved pointing out to the teacher her inappropriate behavior; instead, the consultant should probably use the referred children for his initial intervention locus. For example, instead of telling the teacher that she uses too many negative remarks, it could be pointed out that the child referred has a background of failure and frustration and might thrive on positive attention by the teacher.

While the use of randomization for the selection of the experimental teachers confounded our problems, the reliance upon volunteers can present difficulties with regular classroom teachers. They often reach such a point of frustration that they resist working with the child in any way, saying that an emotionally disturbed child belongs in a special setting and not in a regular classroom, or they wish the consultant to "cure" the child for them.

A basic problem which might be encountered in any behavior modification study is that of finding the appropriate reinforcers for each child. Although this matter was constantly pursued with the teachers in our study, they were reluctant to examine what was important to their students and preferred to accept the suggestions of the researchers at face value. They did not investigate any further whether the back-ups were relevant to the children or not. It is understandable that a teacher cannot evaluate the most fitting reinforcers for each child in the class, but they are certainly better equipped to supply suggestions than are consultants who have little contact with the students.

It should be pointed out that some of our results were fortuitous. For example, one consultant suggested that a teacher respond positively toward a boy's behavior whenever she could and praise his neighbor when the target child misbehaved. The teacher was shown baseline data indicating her reliance upon negative reinforcement. Although this first-year teacher had experienced an unusually bitter introduction to teaching, she agreed to cooperate with the consultant when the intervention period was to begin a few days hence. In the interim a student broke the teacher's nose when she attempted to prevent his damaging school property. A second experimental teacher, who appeared to be successful with her intervention technique, quit her job and the consultant had little success in working with the numerous substitution teachers who followed her.

Outside of those difficulties concerning the teachers, there were school problems which also arose. The school had recently been reopened and was poorly equipped in the way of classroom materials. This handicapped the teachers as well as the pupils, since the teachers found it increasingly difficult to plan their lessons. In a short time, the teachers began to react typically to the behaviors of children, often shouting at them, rather than initiating their behaviors and acting in a consistent fashion. The situation so deteriorated in several experimental classrooms that the initial plan to intervene with two target children per classroom was abandoned in favor of a total classroom intervention.

In the future, it might be possible to arrange contingencies for the teachers themselves, making the intervention program worthwhile to them. Perhaps by cooperating with the Board of Education, researchers in the area of classroom management can provide demonstration teachers with special courses as a possible solution to the many problems encountered in situations of this kind.

Teaching Strategies for Preventing Everyday Problems

The following procedures for classroom management are intended as a guide for the teacher to better enable his students to function at a level appropriate to the objective at hand, namely, education. These procedures have been established by Becker, Thomas and Carnine (1971).

1. Specify in a positive way the rules which are the basis for your reinforcement. Demonstrate the behaviors you desire by praising the children who are good examples of following the rules. Rules are made important to children by providing reinforcement for following the rules. Rules may be different for different work, study, or play periods. Keep the rules to five or six.
2. Relate the children's performance to the rules. Be specific about the behaviors children show which mean "paying attention" or "working hard." "That's a good answer. You listened very closely to my question." Don't be afraid to have fun with your children when the work period is over.
3. Catch the children being good. Reinforce behavior incompatible with that you wish to eliminate. Select incompatible behaviors to reinforce which will be most beneficial to the child's development. Focus on reinforcing tasks important for social and cognitive skills in the process of eliminating disruptive behaviors.
4. Ignore disruptive behaviors unless someone is getting hurt. Focus your attention on the children who are working well to prompt the correct behaviors in the children who are misbehaving. Reinforce improvement when it does occur.
5. When you see a persistent problem behavior, look for the reinforcing events. It may be your own behavior.
6. You can use as a reinforcer any activity the child likes to participate in, as well as social attention, praise, or more tangible reinforcers.
7. Reinforcing events must immediately follow the behavior to be strengthened.
8. Social reinforcers do not work for all children. When necessary to get appropriate behavior going, strengthen the reinforcers being used.
9. Seek special training or consultation if elaborate token systems seem to be the answer for you.
10. Punishment is most likely to be required when the unwanted behavior is very intense or very frequent.
11. If punishment is necessary, first try isolating the child in a room by

himself with only a chair and a light. The child should remain in the time out room until he is quiet for several minutes. Give one warning prior to the use of time out, so that the warning signal can be used most of the time as a punishment without the need for time out.

12. Any use of punishment should be accompanied by the use of reinforcement of behaviors incompatible with the punished behaviors.
13. Hold consistently to your rules for reinforcement, extinction, or punishment. Only if you show consistent reactions to the children's behaviors can they learn what is reinforced and what is not.

Commonly Used Strategies

Some of the most commonly used general strategies of behavior modification used in schools are: (1) extinction and positive reinforcement of incompatible behavior, (2) modeling, role playing and positive reinforcement, and (3) behavior contracts and positive reinforcement. This section will discuss under what conditions these strategies are most likely to be applied. A brief commentary then follows on some of the more common and bothersome school problems with some suggested approaches at solutions.

The combined use of extinction and positive reinforcement of incompatible behavior is probably the most widely used behavioral strategy employed in misconduct situations. Each procedure is more effective when used together than when applied separately. Modeling and role playing share some characteristics, yet differ in others. Modeling suggests that the teacher, through observational learning on the child's part, can promote behavior not in the student's repertoire, change maladaptive behavior, or promote behavior that is inhibited by fear or anxiety. The rationale for role playing is based on the theory that when a student or a teacher assumes a new or different role from his expected behavior, then the behavior of others tends to alter to meet the new role demands. Role playing can be used quite effectively in situations where the child is experiencing disturbed interpersonal relations with his teacher or peers. Moedling can be utilized at a less conscious level, while role playing requires the active cooperation of the student. Positive reinforcement is used with both methods to facilitate the acquisition of new behaviors (Blackham, 1969). Behavioral and academic contracts can be particularly effective with children who are manipulative or lacking in adequate behavioral controls (Keirsey, 1969). A major advantage of this technique is that the child is made aware that the teacher knows why he is behaving in a certain manner.

Techniques for Specific Behavioral Problems

Kennedy (1965) has reported that *school phobia* occurs in about seventeen cases per thousand of school-age children. His intervention approach included the insistence that parents ignore all somatic complaints relating to school avoidance. Results showed no recurrence of the phobia nor substitute symptoms in any of the fifty cases. All of his cases were considered due to neurotic crises. He calls a second type of school phobia *chronic*. It appears in families where at least one parent has serious emotional problems, and is much more difficult to assist because one or both parents refuse to cooperate with any attempts to help. The author encountered a school phobic child his first day of teaching. The student, moderately retarded, refused to return to school after summer vacation because his old classmates had always kidded him about being "slow and stupid." After the boy left, I explained to the class that we should welcome him next time. His mother again brought him the following morning, the class appeared very happy to see him, and he reluctantly stayed. Within a week he had formed a close attachment to the shop teacher who made him a valued aide in preparing and cleaning up materials for class. The boy then became the first student at school each morning and "official greeter" for the remainder of the year.

Because of the arbitrarily imposed restrictions our society has placed on the male and the female "role," so-called *"effeminate" behavior* in a young boy can sometimes disturb the adults in his social environment. If he is ostracized or rejected by these adults, the child can become very confused and unhappy. I once taught in a residential school for children who were labeled as having schizophrenic tendencies. The residential workers were uniformly warm and accepting with all the children except Charles, a very obese, unhappy, and "effeminate" boy. He irritated me too at first because he had a tantrum whenever he didn't get his way, and often refused to work—his excuse was that his therapist had told him he had "excess energy." I taught Charles to do push-ups to assist in ridding him of his obesity problem, and brought a rubber dumbbell set to class from the gym, and explained to Charles that whenever he felt the need for an outlet for his excess energy, he was free to go to the back corner and exercise. Charles was quickly and miraculously "cured" of his excess energy, and with the increased time he could spend on his school work, he soon made surprising academic progress, which was very reinforcing to both Charles and to his teacher. With his exercise activities, Charles began to overcome his obesity (about which he had apparently been very self-conscious), and to learn various athletic and self-defense skills. This led to a new appreciation of Charles by his peers, the staff, and especially by himself—a happier and slimmer Charles.

Burns (1970) devised a similar treatment plan for a third-grade boy who had not been exposed to socially acceptable "male" behavior: encouragement of sports activities, enhancement of the boy's modeling behavior of the typical male role and greater involvement of the child's teacher. Teacher and parents' reports indicated more acceptable behavior. Myrick (1970) also stressed sports activities, but included a male student to act as a model and partner in class events.

Aggressive, acting-out behavior continues to cause more concern for teachers than any other behavior. Mallick and McCandles (1966) have suggested that aggression sometimes increases because children have not been taught to discriminate when it is an appropriate response. They believe that when children are taught, there tends to be a decrease in aggressive behavior.

Glavin and Witt (1969) described a recreation program for extreme acting-out boys in which they were taught to discriminate when a response was appropriate to the school situation. Initially, the content of the recreation program was designed to aid in channeling certain behaviors, such as defiance and aggression, and in preventing others, such as hyperactivity and boisterousness. Wrestling and other activities involving direct physical contact and aggression had not been part of the unstructured recreation program. The behavioral consequences of turning loose our hyperactive and overly aggressive children, for example, in a free play wrestling session had necessitated the elimination of this type of activity from our program. The basic philosophy in the elimination of activities containing a high probability of aggressive contact had been that by not allowing the behavior, we would minimize the possibility that it would, despite our best efforts, be rewarding. This was not found to be true.

When we instituted the structured approach to recreation programing, aggressive activities were included on the assumption that the provision for such behavior in a controlled environment enabled the expression and relearning of aggressive overt physical activities through outlets in acceptable behavioral channels. It was found that certain activities, such as wrestling, stunts, and soccer, allowed for "legalized" aggressive behavior—situations where aggression was an accepted but controlled part of the play environment.

In all of these activities certain rules and procedures were instituted to insure control over deviant behavior. In the wrestling phase of the program, participants were required to go through specified warm up calisthenics before beginning the actual wrestling. This procedure established leader control over the situation and made it clear that the wrestling to follow was a part of a total physical activities program rather than simply a chance for masked aggression. During the wrestling sessions, two boys participated at a time while a third acted as referee. The other boys were asked to sit quietly along the side of the mat. This rule was found to be necessary to control excessive excitement which easily turned to anger on the part of wrestlers and observers. Their participation in the remaining wrestling matches that day was contingent upon their obeying this rule. During the match the child who acted as referee made all decisions as to when participants were off the mat, when an illegal hold was being used, and when one participant had held the other down for a ten-count. The adult recreation leader controlled the length of time that the match proceeded and gave general instructions as to wrestling rules and techniques.

At the end of the match, both participants were required to shake hands signifying the end of the match and the true play nature of their wrestling aggression. If they were unwilling to shake hands, they were not to participate in additional matches that day. This never occurred. The appropriate use of aggressive behavior was reinforced by the "transference" of quarrels occurring at other times in the day to the structured wrestling program during the noon hour recreation. Boys involved in previous arguments would be allowed a normal period of wrestling after they had first warmed up with a few "strenuous excerises." The exertion demanded by the excercises helped to keep the wrestling session within specified behavioral bounds by syphoning off most of the boys' destructive energy.

The use of time-out is another approach for curbing acting out behavior. Several recent projects dealing with severe acting-out children have used a small enclosed cubicle at the side of the classroom called a time-out room. This room contains no objects of interest and prevents the child from receiving peer attention. Most studies report that the child should remain in the time-out room for a specified time after he regains control—usually ten minutes. Sulzer, Mayer and Cody (1968) and Pendergrass (1970) have reported that this procedure can be very valuable in decreasing acting-out behavior. The author's own experience with time-out rooms suggests several modifications with the procedure. A cubicle is often not neccesary and even impractical; instead, seat the child in a corner of the room so that he can observe the classroom activities but where his classmates are not facing him; the rationale being that the teacher has made his classroom an exciting and interesting place and the disruptive child can see what positive reinforcements he is missing. If the time-outs are issued early in the disrupting act, before it has time to build up, then the time outs will generally be short and the amount of contagion minimal. It helps to curtail the specified time the child needs to show regained self-control to perhaps even one minute; the aim is to have the child return to purposeful activity as soon as possible and to minimize the disrupting event. Finally, the teacher should not scold the child either while administering the time-out or after it is completed.

Occasionally even the application of the time-out procedure will not stop the child from being a disrupting influence on the class. Kiersey (1969) and other professionals have suggested the use of systematic suspension or exclusion. It requires an agreement between the teacher, principal and parents that the child will be excluded from school for a specified period of time with the parents not scolding the child, but barring him from his normal attractive activities. There are several problems with this approach. Often the parents will not be cooperative and will even be hostile toward the school authorities for requiring them to come to school to remove or return their child. Parents frequently will scold their child but will not supervise his behavior during the suspension time to exclude him from participating in reinforcing activities. Finally, the use of this technique removes the child from purposeful, educational experiences for a longer time than is often necessary. In its place, I would recommend sending the continuously disrupting child to a room with neutral stimulus properties. A school official such as the principal, secretary, counselor, nurse or others should be present but should continue to attend to his own work rather than interact with the child. No counseling or requests for explanations from the child should be made at this time; instead, the child should be presented with the academic task he normally would be doing at that time. When the child has completed the task, he should not be given positive reinforcement or tokens if he is on a token economy; rather, he should be given the opportunity to return to his room with the completed work assignment. During the time the child is sent out of the classroom, until he returns to the room, the atmosphere should be kept as unemotional and nonjudgmental as possible. Normally, this procedure will suffice for most crisis situations. If not, only then should systematic suspension be used.

The problem of children who are *truant* can often be curtailed if a token reinforcement system is successfully applied in the classroom. This may require placing the child in a self-contained special class; placement in a resource room for part of the school day may not be sufficient, for the child may become truant for all but the resource room period.

Another method recommended by Blackham and Silberman (1971) is called the "triangle method" and essentially involves placing the truant child in a group with two non-truant children who are his friends. The group is placed on a reinforcement system whereby they can earn tokens only if all members of the group are present.

An *excessively boisterous class* can present difficulties for the teacher, his colleagues and school administrators. Smith and Smith (1966), Hunter (1967) and Barrish, Saunders and Wolf (1969) have reported successful behavior modification approaches to this problem. In our research (Glavin, Quay and Werry, 1971) we found it necessary to attempt a "whispering rule" in two classes for acting-out children. After the initial shock wore off, one class was soon as noisy as ever. After observing a short time in this class, the problem was found to be that the teacher, teacher aide and other adult visitors to the class were talking in a normally pitched voice. After the adult behavior was changed, a change in the behavior of the students soon followed. The classroom atmosphere quickly shifted to one of peacefulness and productivity. An interesting sidelight was that while the number of time-outs remained the same—mainly given for breaking the whispering rule—their duration was much shorter, and the nature of the offenses requiring a time-out was much milder. These results suggest again that the teacher should intervene as early as possible with a disruptive child rather than waiting for his behavior to build up or incite his classmates.

Conclusion

In most of the interventions described in this book, some person, stimulus or technique is temporarily added to or substracted from the student's school environment in order to directly influence specific aspects of the child's classroom behavior. One of the most widely accepted techniques for helping behavior problem children has been the use of peers or adults to act as teacher aides. Their role has been primarily that of contributing their knowledge or skill in specific situations to the disturbed child's development. The primary sources of manpower for the role of teacher aides have been the child's peers from his classroom, older students, adult volunteers from the community, paid teacher assistants, and parents. If parents are utilized, it is generally advisable that they not be assigned to their own child's classroom.

Stimuli may be manipulated in various ways to assist the behavior problem child. Appropriate models can be provided for the child. New learning experiences or educational innovations which rely on different sensory stimulations can be employed which aid the child's growth in particular deficit areas. Numerous types of contingency-contracting or self-management systems can be attempted in order to motivate the child to compete with either himself or his peers. Other interventions might include the reduction of stimuli for the problem child. These include the use of student cubicles, time-outs, removal to another section of the school building for cooling-off purposes, shortened school days or temporary school exclusion in extreme cases.

By far the most important technique discussed has been the systematic application of positive reinforcement to change disturbed children's behavior. These techniques will usually be more effective if applied in conjunction with the interventions described in other sections of the book, particularly the "Individualization and Structure" chapter. Specific positive reinforcement techniques that have been successfully utilized are verbal reinforcement, teacher attention, various signals such as buzzers or lights to indicate appropriate behavior, special privileges normally found in the classroom environmant, or, if all else fails, token economies which use extrinsic rewards as backup reinforcers.

References

Barrish, H. H., M. Saunders and M. M. Wolf. "Good behavior game: Effects of individual contingencies for group consequences on disruptive behavior in a classroom." *Journal of Applied Behavior Analysis*, (1969), *2*, 119–24.

Becker, W. C., D. R. Thomas and D. Carnine. *Reducing behavior problems: An operant conditioning guide for teachers.* National Laboratory on Early Childhood Education, Urbana, Illinois, 1969.

Blackham, G. J. "Strategies for change in the child client." *Elementary School Guidance and Counseling* (1969), *3*, 174–81.

Blackham, G. J. and A. Silberman. *Modification of child behavior.* Belmont, California: Wadsworth Publishing Co., 1971.

Burns, B. "Jim: The case of an effeminate boy." Unpublished manuscript. Tempe Elementary Schools, Tempe, Arizona, 1970.

Glavin, J. P., H. C. Quay, R. F. Annesley and J. S. Werry. "An experimental resource room program for classroom behavior problem children." *Exceptional Children* (1971), *38*, 131–37.

Glavin, J. P., H. C. Quay and J. S. Werry. "Behavioral and academic gains of conduct problem children in different classroom settings." *Exceptional Children* (1971), *37*, 441–46.

Glavin, J. P. and P. Witt. "Recreation for the conduct disorder child." *Exceptional Children* (1969), *35*, 787–91.

Hunter, M. *Reinforcement theory for teachers.* El Segundo, California: Tip Publications, 1967.

Keirsey, D. W. "Systematic exclusion: Eliminating chronic classroom disruptions." In J. D. Krumboltz and C. E. Thoresen (eds.), *Behavioral counseling, case studies and techniques.* New York: Holt, Rinehart and Winston, 1969. 89–113.

Kennedy, W. A. "School phobia: Rapid treatment of fifty cases." *Journal of Abnormal Psychology* (1965), *70*, 285–89.

Long, N. J., W. C. Morse and R. G. Newman. *Conflict in the classroom: The education of emotionally disturbed children.* Belmont, California: Wadsworth Publishing Co., 1965.

Mallick, S. K. and B. R. McCandles. "A study of catharsis of aggression." *Journal of Personality and Social Psychology* (1966), *4*, 591–96.

Myrick, R. D. "The counselor–consultant and the effeminate boy." *Personnel and Guidance Journal* (1970), *45*, 351–61.

Pendergrass, V. Children and behavior modification: Time-out from positive reinforcement as a punishment procedure. Paper read at Florida Psychological Association, May 1, 1970, Miami, Florida.

Quay, H. C., J. P. Glavin, F. M. Davis, and M. Mishkin. "The education of behaviorally disordered children in the public school setting: Behavioral consulting to regular classroom teachers: A pilot study." U. S. Office of Education Grant No. OEG-3-6-062063-1559(032), 1971.

Smith, J. M. and E. P. Smith. *Child management: A program for parents and teachers.* Ann Arbor, Michigan: Ann Arbor Publishers, 1966.

Sulzer, B., A. R. Mayer, and J. J. Cody, "Assisting teachers with managing classroom behavioral problems." *Elementary School Guidance and Counseling* (1968), *3*, 40–48. Thomas, D.R., W.C. Becker, and M. Armstrong. "Production and elimination of disruptive classroom behavior by systematically varying teacher's behavior." *In Operant Conditioning in the classroom: Introductory Readings in Educational Psychology.* C. E. Pitts, ed. New York: T.Y. Crowell. 1971. 166–83.

3

Behavior Modification As Applied Today

The purpose of this chapter is to present an overview of the most common behavior modification techniques presently used in classrooms. Emphasis will be placed upon supplying a detailed description of the most popular behavioral technique adopted by teachers: token reinforcement programs with extrinsic back-up reinforcers. These approaches are not exhaustive of possible behavior modification approaches which can be applied in the classroom, nor are they substitutions for the innovative and creative techniques which each teacher naturally develops through experience.

Behavior modification uses the systematic application of learning theory deduced from experimental research to change some observable behavior. Although research in applied behavior modification for the classroom has expanded greatly, the interested teacher or beginning practitioner may not have ready access to the journals, or perhaps, of greater importance, he may not be sophisticated in the basic modification often needed by the classroom teacher to successfully apply research results.

Recent History

Behavioral analysis, consequence management, or behavior modification has its roots with the behavioral learning theorists Thorndike, Pavlov, Watson, and Jones. Ayllon (1965) and Ferster and Skinner (1957) expanded and refined the theory and popularized its clinical use, enabling the behavioral specialist to use it in modifying deviant behavior. Clinical experimentation with individual children and adults brought this approach into the foregraound in the 1960s. Since then, the application of behavioral techniques for changing academic or social behavior of students has expanded rapidly.

Behavior modification is a systematic, highly structured approach to altering behavior. Presented below is a list of the various techniques. These techniques will have the effect of strengthening, weakening or maintaining target behavior. For a more detailed description, refer to Reese (1966) and Nesworth, Deno, and Jenkins (1969).

Basic Definitions

Behavior modification can be defined as an attempt to change a certain type of behavior using various procedures which either strengthen or weaken the behavior. Some methods that are used to modify behavior are conditioning, shaping, reinforcement, and extinction. Conditioning is the process of developing within the organism a specific response to a specific stimulus. Shaping involves the rewarding or reinforcement for every response that is made; that is, in the direction of the desired behavioral goal. Reinforcements can be defined as any stimuli which increase the probability that the desired behavior will be performed in the future. This can be used in establishing more firmly existing patterns of behavior or in facilitating newly developing patterns of behavior. Extinction is the opposite of reinforcement. Extinction occurs when a reinforcement is withheld on such conditions that the behavior no longer happens.

Consequences which strengthen behavior are called reinforcers. A positive reinforcer may be any event which strengthens desired behavior. A reinforcer strengthens a response in the sense that it increases the probability that the response will occur again (Reese, 1966). Reinforcers can be used to strengthen or weaken existing behavior. Reinforcements can be adapted not only for promoting behavior development, but also for increasing academic progress.

The various types of reinforcement are positive, negative, direct and vicarious. Generally speaking, reinforcements in the category of praise and approval are positive in nature, while those involving reproof, punishment and disapproval are negative in nature. Many things are taken into consideration when deciding the reinforcement value and whether or not it is positive or negative in nature. Something a teacher does may be positively reinforcing in one instance but negatively reinforcing in another. Doing or saying nothing to the learner may, in fact, have positive or negative reinforcing value, depending on the circumstances. Positive reinforcement may take the form of praise, reward, privilege or admiration. Negative reinforcements may take the form of punishment, disciplinary action, social ostracization, or withdrawal of the reinforcement.

An example of direct reinforcement would be outward praise for a child. Direct reinforcement is on a one-to-one basis. Those involved are the person giving praise and the one being praised. Vicarious reinforcement occurs during direct praise. The actions taken when direct reinforcement is being used will have an effect on the people surrounding the person being reinforced. They will see what is happening to him for a particular behavior, and depending on whether the reinforcement is positive or negative for them, will either imitate or refrain from that particular behavior.

Behavior Modification Procedures

Rewarding a desired response has the effect of strengthening that response and is called *positive reinforcement*. The reward may be a primary reinforcer such as food or it may be a secondary reinforcer such as social praise, a gummed star, or a hug. This technique is especially effective in developing and maintaining desirable behavior. One problem the teacher may encounter is getting the child to initially emit the positive response. The method for doing this is called shaping or successive approximation, whereby the teacher separates the desired behavior into a hierarchy of responses and begins with the easiest response. For instance, if you want to strengthen speech development in the child, start by rewarding every vocal utterance. Then you might reward only those sounds which appear in the English language. Finally, give reinforcement only for meaningful words used appropriately. It is obvious that this is a simple example; the effective use of shaping requires knowledge of the developmental stages involved in the desired behavior. The teacher wants to develop and *maintain* desirable behavior. Initially, the reinforcement schedule will be continuous and consistent and the rewards will most likely be physical or tangible in nature. Once the behavior has developed, reinforcement is given intermittantly or inconsistently. The ultimate goals of this technique are: (1) to work on an intermittant reinforcement schedule, and (2) to work for social reinforcers.

Extinction is a technique used to decrease or eliminate disturbing behavior, and is facilitated by the consistent withdrawal of reinforcers. Clarizio and Yelon (1971) noted that this procedure was effective with such behaviors as excessive talking, tantrum behavior and academic errors. Teachers will recognize that extinction is frequently not the most economical and efficient procedure for the classroom. Behavior that is destructive to others or to self simply cannot be ignored. Not only can harm be done to the child and to others, but other children may be seduced into imitating the behavior, thus adding a contagion factor. Extinction does not always permanently eliminate the problem behavior, and at a later time the procedure may have to be reinstituted. Furthermore, some behaviors just won't be extinguished, whether or not positive reinforcement is withdrawn. The child who sucks his thumb or physically stimulates himself will continue the behavior because positive reinforcement is built into the act.

Assume that a child who finds arithmetic unrewarding leaves his seat excessively during the lesson. The teacher has attempted to eliminate this behavior by using extinction but the procedure has not been effective. Someone would inevitably yell "sit down" the child would receive the desired attention, and out-of-seat behavior would be reinforced.

An alternative technique involves *reinforcing incompatible responses* to the bothersome behavior. This same teacher decides to reward the child for completing ten arithmetic problems. In order to accomplish this task and obtain the reward, the child is too busy to walk around the room. The desired behavior is incompatible with out-of-seat behavior. Not only does this approach reduce disturbing behavior, but it also increases desirable academic performance. Although reinforcing incompatible responses has not received as much emphasis as other behavioral techniques, it appears to be a most applicable and effective procedure for classroom use.

Children sometimes commit disruptive behavior because they have failed to learn in which situations certain responses are or are not, appropriate (i.e., *discrimination learning*). This results in overgeneralization of behavior. (Yelling aloud to gain attention may be appropriate at home or on the playground, but is bothersome and inappropriate in the classroom.) The teacher begins the process of discrimination learning by labeling a certain behavior as appropriate or inappropriate within the classroom setting. Using the above illustration, he might inform the child that, while yelling is acceptable on the playground, children do not yell out in class. If they want attention they must raise their hand and be called on.

Follow-up is usually necessary whereby the teacher discourages inappropriate behavior while reinforcing appropriate responses. The teacher must remember that certain desired behaviors are peculiar *only* to the classroom, and thus, must be taught.

Desensitization is a technique which is used primarily with the extremely fearful or phobic child. The aim of the process is to have the child develop a relaxed response in a situation which previously produced anxiety or fear. By developing a hierarchy of acts involved in completing the behavior, starting with the least threatening one, the child slowly approximates the fearful response. Frequently each approximation is accompanied by a reward, thus making the behavior more tolerable.

Modeling holds that a behavior pattern, once acquired through imitation, is often maintained without deliberate external reinforcement. Children acquire much of their behavior by modeling or imitating the behavior of others. You may see young children at play dressing up like mommy or daddy and role playing their routines. This is an obvious example of modeling. Similarly, teachers have considerable influence in affecting the acquisition of new behaviors through imitation. There are three major effects of modeling: (1) the modeling effect, (2) the inhibitory effect and (3) the eliciting effect (Bandura, 1965). With the modeling effect, the child acquires a new response which is not present in his repertoire of behaviors. The inhibitory (or disinhibitory) effect is the strengthening or weakening of previously punished responses which are already a part of the child's behavioral pattern. Clarizio and McCoy (1970) offer an example of this effect. "Children who see an age-mate punished or rewarded for aggressive behavior tend to decrease or increase their behavior accordingly" (p. 452). When the behavior is neither new nor previously punished and occurs in response to the teacher's discriminating cues, it is considered to have an eliciting effect. For the success of the modeling technique, the teacher must have the attention of the child, for without this, no predetermined effects can take place. The teacher must be aware of the complexity of the stimulus. Can the child imitate the behavior or does it need to be broken down into smaller components? Finally, the model should be a prestigious figure to the child.

Punishment consists in the presentation of either physically or psychologically painful stimuli or the withdrawal of pleasant stimuli when undesirable behavior occurs. When negative reinforcement (punishment) is the consequence of a certain action, it has the effect of arresting or suppressing that behavior, without eliminating or extinguishing it. It is beneficial only when applied to specific acts (running out into the street) rather than global situations (being a naughty child). Momentarily stopping undesirable behavior has positive effects when it is accompanied by the demonstration and reinforcement of appropriate alternative responses. The teacher must be aware of the possible negative aspects of punishment. Emotional side effects—guilt, fear, withdrawal, and frustration may lead to other maladaptive behaviors. In addition, the punishing teacher may serve as a negative, aggressive model for the children.

Implementation of Behavioral Procedures

In order to employ a behavior modification procedure effectively, it is necessary for the teacher to have a basic understanding of which consequences increase, eliminate, or maintain behaviors. This section details the steps required in applying contingency management.

First, pinpoint the target behavior. By observing the children, note the behaviors that need to be modified. The target behaviors may involve the entire class or may be limited to one or two pupils. This selection must meet the three criteria of specificity, countability and directionality. Avoid choosing a behavior that is vague or general. The target behavior should be stated precisely and explicitly; it should include a clearly specified criterion of occurrence or nonoccurence so that other observers could reliably count it. It is desirable to consider the possibilities of reinforcing incompatible responses, such as increasing the completion of academic seatwork, rather than decreasing out-of-seat behavior. After listing the behaviors, relist them in order of urgency and treat the first one immediately. Consider whether the behavior is truly undesirable and determine if expectations for change are realistic for the age of the pupil(s) and the situation.

Then, collect the baseline data. This procedure involves counting the frequency of occurrence prior to treatment and enables the observer to determine the extent of the behavior and eventually evaluate the results of the program. Data collection should not be restricted to one or two observations, nor to one specific time each day. Rather, the behaviors should be recorded in as many situations as possible and as frequently as possible. From this baseline data a teacher not only determines that fighting is a real problem, but he also knows that its occurrence is greatest during reading. At this point, it is most efficient to observe the students during the reading period and collect data at this given time.

Third, select reinforcers. Reinforcers, i.e. consequences, are often considered reasons for doing something. In other words, behavior is to a large extent, greatly influenced by its consequences. In modifying a behavior it is essential to find a consequence which is highly appealing to the pupil. Several methods for determining an effective reinforcer are: observing the child to see what he enjoys, asking the child what he likes best, and presenting a few objects from which he may choose. It should be reemphasized here that one of the goals of behavior modification is encouraging a child or class of children to work for social reinforcement and self-management. Thus, whenever food or toys are given as a consequence, they must be accompanied by a social reinforcement—verbal praise, a smile, a star, or a hug. Eventually, the social reinforcement will have the same effect as a tangible item. A large variety of back-up reinforcers should be provided so as to decrease the possibility of satiation. This sometimes means searching for reinforcers not normally found in the typical classroom, but whenever possible, the teacher should utilize natural reinforcers, those normally found in the school.

The fourth step is to initiate the contingency program. The essence of the intervention is contingency contracting, whereby the teacher specifies the task or behavior the children must perform and the reinforcers their accomplishment will receive. This means that if you do X, you will get Y. There are at least two approaches available to the manager seeking to alter behavior. First, he might consider what has already been attempted; perhaps one of these procedures was more effective than another, in which case that procedure could be renewed. It is possible that many of the enviromental alterations or rules that the teacher has attempted, had they been consistently and continuously followed, would successfully control the behavior of children. Therefore, only this one change, and no others, should be attempted for a few days. A second source for the manager to consider when seeking a procedure for change is his past experience. Perhaps a third source for remediation guidance would be to consult other managers who may have successfully dealt with similar problems. Regardless of the source, changes should be placed in effect over a period of days reinforcing successive approximations to change the child's behavior.

Fifth, evaluate the treatment program. In evaluation, the utilization of a frequency graph eliminates confusion and subjectivity. Extending the horizontal axis allows for a daily record of treatment data. Glancing at the graph, it becomes apparent whether or not the treatment has been effective. The teacher may conclude that the treatment has been successful; he can now aim at stabilizing and maintaining the behavior. This may involve changing the reinforcers, the schedule of reinforcement, or the behavior criterion. On the basis of the data, the manager must decide whether to continue the treatment procedure with the initial environmental change in effect, or to try another. If the decision is to try a different procedure, this change too must be placed in effect for a long period of time to assess its function. If the intervention proves to be less than satisfying, he may wish to examine whether the approximations are too steep, the reinforcements too inadequate, the tasks too generalized or too difficult, or the payoff too delayed. These are all fairly common mistakes made by beginning practitioners of behavior modification.

Finally, generalize the behavior. The final step of the treatment program is generalizing the results to other situations and other modes of reinforcement. This can be accomplished by using one or more of the following procedures:

1. Place the behavior on intermittant reinforcement.
2. Fade the reinforcer from primary to social.
3. Have another adult (parent, another teacher) participate in the treatment.
4. Stress reinforcement of academic rather than behavioral change.
5. Contract with the student to monitor his behavior by keeping his own record and turning it in at the end of the week for reinforcement.
6. Use tokens to bridge the gap between primary and social reinforcement and to encourage delay in gratification.

It is understandable that the time requirements for these procedures appear to be lengthy. They are essential, however, for successful application. Also, once these procedures have been practiced, their time efficiency increases markedly. The following action research is an example of a teacher's application of behavior modification principles while learning about the subject in a college credit course.

Reduction of Interrupting Behavior in First Grade Children

by

Libby Goodman

The program of the transition class which I teach at the Rosemont Elementary School in the Radnor Township District is highly diversified to meet the variety of social, emotional and academic needs of my children. To the greatest extent possible, the work is individualized. Typically, the first part of the morning is devoted to math and reading activities and the teacher works with individuals or small groups rather than the whole class. However, this teacher found it very difficult to carry out an individualized program because of the constant interruptions. These interruptions were, in most instances, unnecessary, distracting to the teacher and the child or group of children she was working with, and time consuming. Thus, the goal for this action research project became a reduction in the frequency of interrupting behaviors during a thirty-minute morning work period.

Subjects. Twelve children in the self-contained transition class were the subjects for this project. The subjects were all six years of age, with the exception of one child who was seven. All of the subjects possessed average or above intellectual ability. The class was comprised of nine boys and three girls.

Procedure. The morning routine during a structured work period consisted of the following: work was distributed, instructions (verbal or demonstration) were given, and all questions were answered. The children were expected to attend to the instructions. If they had a question after the work period had begun they were to ask a neighbor for help before coming to the teacher. After their work was completed, the children were free to choose a spare-time activity from a wide variety of materials available in the classroom. Additional measures were also instituted to eliminate the need for coming to the teacher. Drink and bathroom passes were available so that a child needed only to take a pass to leave the room. Extra pencils, erasers, crayons, and paper were openly available at all times. Nevertheless, some interruptions were necessary. Children were not penalized in these instances.

Baseline data was gathered for a period of five days during the first thirty-minute work period of the day. The teacher tried to adhere as closely as possible to the time span between 9:30 and 10:00 o'clock each morning. The treatment was begun on the sixth day. If a child interrupted the teacher needlessly, a mark was recorded on the teacher's tally sheet next to the child's name. The teacher would also say, "I'm sorry but I'll have to count this an interruption." However, the teacher would always indicate to the child what he should have done instead of interruption. A six year old child not only needs to be told that he has acted inappropriately; he needs to be told the appropriate course of action as well.

At the end of the thirty-minute period, a star was given to each child who had not excessively interrupted the teacher and the children she was working with. The number of interruptions allowed was gradually reduced until one interruption was the maximum number for all of the children. The stars were pasted on a poster by each child's name. On Friday, the children with enough stars were allowed to pick a prize. The prizes consisted of pencils, crayons, chalk, balloons, note pads, marbles, tootsie toy cards, plastic easter eggs, library passes, and so forth. The prices for these items ranged from nothing to a maximum of ten cents. The daily distribution of stars took approximately five minutes. On Friday, fifteen minutes were allotted for the final tally and selection of prizes.

Results and Discussion. The treatment was effective in reducing the amount of interrupting behavior in a group of twelve transition-class youngsters. During the five-day baseline period, the mean number of interruptions was 18.60. During the four consecutive five-day periods in which the treatment was applied, the mean number of interruptions steadily decreased (8.12; 3.60; 3.20; 3.00).

One modification in the system has already been initiated. Disruptive behavior anywhere in the classroom, which causes the teacher to shift her attention from the child or group that she is working with comes under the classification of "interruption." Thus a wider range of behaviors has been brought under the control of the system. In addition, the teacher plans to lengthen the work period to forty or forty-five minutes and to initiate a second structured work period in either the morning or afternoon.

Token Economies

When teachers hear of behavior modification, some sort of token economy usually comes to mind. Indeed, the results of research demonstrate that token economies are effective. Their application in the regular classroom, however, is questionable, especially if consulting support is unavailable. As mentioned before, extensive training for teachers would be necessary. Also, a great deal of materials would be needed including things to use as tokens, and candy, toys, etc., to give in exchange for the tokens. Even if special privileges are granted in place of giving out objects, extra personnel might be necessary to monitor the activities. Perhaps the most important point to consider, before the implementation of a token program, is whether or not it is actually needed.

There are important points that need to be defined before a token economy program is begun. For example: How many tokens should be rewarded; when should tokens be handed out; and how gradually should the criterion increase as the program progresses? In many research studies these questions were often defined by the experimenter beforehand and simply carried out by the teacher. This again points out the need for extensive training of teachers before running token programs. If training is not provided, outside personnel must come to review the problem. This is a crucial point; a child cannot be kept on token reinforcement indefinitely. Because the world does not operate on immediate reward as in token economies, he must make a transition to normal-type reinforcers, and handling the transition is a delicate task.

Kuypers, Becker and O'Leary (1968) studied some of the problems that arise when a token system is implemented. Their research examined a situation in which the teacher had read about token economies but had no understanding of the underlying principles nor how any additional modifications were made by the teacher in her classroom management. Originally the study intended to include additional phases of teacher training in behavioral techniques, but it had to be abandoned at the teacher's insistence. The major oversights made by this teacher are commonly encountered with naive practitioners: A shaping technique was not used, and social reinforcers were not contingently applied when tokens were awarded, or at other times during the day. This study demonstrated the point that a token system alone cannot serve as the solution for classroom management, and that it should not be applied by the inexperienced teacher without supervision.

Discussion

It has been demonstrated that social incentives and back-up reinforcement are both effective in influencing behavior and motivating learning. The question now becomes: Which is more practical for classroom use? Although effective, back-up reinforcers require elaborate planning for their delivery and exchange. This planning involves criterion for reinforcement, value of tokens, a method of record keeping, a system for exchanging tokens for goods, training of teachers and the handling of the transition period.

Social incentives have proven to be the easiest type of incentive to use in the educational setting. Since social reinforcers are verbal, and since most children seek support and praise from the teacher, social incentives are also the most natural type of reinforcement. Another advantage is that using social incentives allows teachers to modify their own behavior and create a supporting, friendly atmosphere in the classroom.

Quite often, operant principles can be successfully used in the classroom outside the framework of a token economy. Only when this does not prove feasible, should a token economy be attempted, using naturalistic back-up reinforcements first and extrinsic reinforcers as a final measure. It must be emphasized that employing operant procedures alone will not act as a panacea for classroom problems; individualized instruction, continuous data collection and evaluation of procedures, to name but a few methods, are equally necessary.

References

Ayllon, T. "Intensive treatment of psychotic behavior by stimulus satiation and food reinforcement." In L. P. Ullmann and L. Krasner (eds.), *Case studies in behavior modification*. New York: Holt, Rinehart and Winston, 1965.

Bandura, A. "Behavior modification through modeling procedures." In L. Krasner and L. P. Ullman (eds.), *Research in behavior modification*. New York: Holt, Rinehart and Winston, 1965.

Clarizio, H. F. and S. L. Yelon. "Learning theory approaches to classroom management: Rationale and intervention techniques." In D. D. Hammill and N. R. Bartel (eds.), *Educational perspectives in learning disabilities*. New York: John Wiley, 1971.

Ferster, C. B. and B. F. Skinner. *Schedules of reinforcement*. New York: Appleton-Century-Crofts, 1957.

Kuypers, D. S., W. C. Becker and K. D. O'Leary. "How to make a token system fail." *Exceptional Children* (1968), *35* (2), 101–9.

Neisworth, J. T., S. L. Deno and J. R. Jenkins. *Student motivation and classroom management: A behavioristic approach*. Lemont, Pa.: Behavior Technics, Inc., 1969.

Reese, E. *The analysis of human operant behavior*. Dubuque, Iowa: Brown and Co., 1966.

4

Some Reflections on Behavior Modification in the Classroom

In its effort to improve learning, education has focused on the science of human behavior, in an attempt to provide an understanding of the individual and, at the same time, find practical methods for the classroom that will facilitate teaching and enhance learning. The use of reinforcement principles to deal with specific behavior problems has been found useful. Despite the apparent simplicity of behavior modification theory and its implementation, our experience (Quay, et al., 1967) and that of others (e.g., Baer, Wolf and Risley, 1968; O'Leary and Drabman, 1971) has revealed a host of problems for the teacher, which are pertinent to program operation in the classroom.

Common Problems in Applying Behavior Modification

A main criticism of behavior modification techniques is that they can extend too far into the extrinsic realm of behavior without considering the equally important intrinsic side. Maer (1968) speaks of limitations regarding the application of reinforcement theory to education. He states that it is not only desirable but *necessary* to find an internal and subjective theory of motivation in order to handle complex human learning. Reinforcement principles, such as the importance of the immediacy of reinforcement and the superiority of positive opposed to negative reinforcement, are just too simple. They will not provide an efficient or easily obtainable solution to the problem of getting the student to confront, persist and learn from the educational task. Maer gives an example concerning misunderstood reinforcement use. He mentions that being right at a task can possibly become boring for the student. Learning must contain the element of challenge. Too often, a steady diet of reinforcement involves little possibility of failure. Success may have satiating effects as well as stimulating ones.

Another misuse of the behavior modification approach is the creation of an unnatural situation in school. School should be as life-like as possible. Because failure is a natural part of life's experiences, programs containing almost total reinforcement can create an artificial condition. Although some students need a great deal of success in their learning experiences, it is also true that they must somehow experience failure to prepare fully for life. Without some failure, success can lose its original meaning. Maer states that potential failure is probably an important ingredient in the learning situation. The reality of failure makes success meaningful and a successfully performed task more interesting.

At the beginning of a classroom program using token reinforcers, immediate delivery of the reinforcers is crucial; having to wait for the reinforcer can be very frustrating for the child. This often presents logistical problems. Teachers need to give help to children and provide instruction as well as disburse reinforcers. Many solutions to this problem have been proposed. A teacher assistant can function solely to assess responses and disburse rewards. Unfortunately, this tends to retard, or perhaps inhibit altogether, the speed with which the teacher's approval actions can become reinforcers themselves. Automation of response counting and reinforcing is a possibility, especially in conjunction with computerized instruction, but the technical problems and costs encountered are likely to be beyond the capabilities of the public schools at the present time. Self-recording and self-reinforcing has also been suggested. Obviously, however, these behaviors must themselves be learned by the children. Opportunities for dissimulation are also inherent and will be readily seen, especially by conduct-problem children. More research is needed in the use of this approach or, at this juncture, it may create more problems than it solves.

Conduct-disorder children frequently develop sets of behaviors which have produced short term gratification from others. Many of these behaviors may be loosely characterized as *manipulative*. Such behaviors will, at least at the outset, be utilized in an attempt to obtain reinforcers without making the appropriate responses. These manipulative responses are already strong ones in the repertoire and frequently require less effort than the "correct" responses. Wheedling, crying, scapegoating, rationalizing, threatening, physically aggressing may all fit this description.

Children are also very clever at finding either logical or mechanical inconsistencies and weaknesses in the administration of the token reinforcement system. The clock system of recording time-on-the-job (Quay, et al.) used in the first year of our research was the frequent object of attempts to "beat the system." When the teacher was at his desk or occupied with another child and less likely to detect deviant behavior, some children would stop work until the teacher noticed. When he moved to stop their clock, they would quickly recommence.

Setting Educational Goals

MacMillan and Forness' article (1970) on the limitations and liabilities of behavior modification reported some of the typical abuses of the approach by "naive" teachers. The first criticism which MacMillan and Forness discuss is that "learning theory does not guide the teacher in determining educational goals" (p. 292). They point out that teachers are often more concerned with behavior than with skill development. It would appear that many behavior modification investigators have tended to set unnecessarily limited goals.

Most teachers, when applying the use of behavior modification principles for the first time, focus on socially disturbed target behaviors. These disturbing behaviors can often be changed indirectly simply by reinforcing improved academic performance. For example, good academic performance early in the morning is incompatible with lateness and acting out behavior; so the latter two variables would improve if the first variable improved. Glavin, Quay and Werry (1971) found that when program emphasis was changed to stress rewards for academic performance, the change not only brought about concomitant gains in academic achievement, but also specific forms of behavior which are related to the learning process. In addition, this approach can involve little additional work in data collection. It is predicted that increased attention to the reinforcement of academic goals will continue and will play a major role in assisting the behavior modification paradigm to gain educational relevance.

Behavioral goals, perhaps as secondary goals, may still be necessary for some children and, no doubt, will continue to be chosen by some teachers. Before berating this practice, one should remember the countless times teachers have reported specific behavioral changes leading to improved peer interactions as well as the pupil–teacher relationship itself. Again, as with academic goals, a strong case can be made for the idea that the teacher, rather than some other professional, is the logical determiner of behavioral goals; he is living with and observing the child, his peers and the situation every day, in a realistic developmental framework. The current trend is toward increasing consideration of the child's rights to participate in choosing the behavioral goal.

Motivation

MacMillan and Forness' second criticism is that relying exclusively on extrinsic reinforcement is too confining—a view which behaviorists would applaud. While the authors acknowledge the shaping principles leading to intrinsic motivation used by behavior modifiers, they advocate other possibilities of motivation. In point of fact, reinforcement techniques properly used can result in the teacher becoming a powerful social reinforcer for the child. Just as importantly, the increasing amounts of effective behavior exhibited by the children can be potent reinforcers for the teachers. Such a dyad of mutual positive reinforcement for effective behavior of both teacher and pupil in the classroom is the essence of a good teacher-pupil relationship. Other intrinsic motivations thought to be overlooked by MacMillan and Forness already have been incorporated into behavior modification research. Free-time activity centers are often utilized by practitioners to capitalize on the child's desire for exploratory behavior. Again, the importance of correctly individualizing the child's curriculum should be emphasized, and also the fact that providing success in intrinsically reinforcing for most children. Finally, curiosity and novelty have been incorporated successfully in reinforcer delivery systems as an added means of motivating conduct-problem children (Glavin, Quay and Werry).

On the other hand, naive practitioners often use token economies with artificial back-up reinforcers without searching for more naturalistic reinforcers or without investigating important factors which could influence the behavior of the student. It is not unusual, unfortunately, for a teacher to continue a token reinforcement system, unchanged, for a year or more without giving any thought to maintaining the new behavior with naturalistic reinforcers, once it has been acquired by utilizing the token economy.

Reinforcement

A lack of responsiveness to the traditional reinforcers of the classroom by the atypical child may initially demand the use of edibles, manipulables or money reinforcers. Indeed, effective reinforcers may have to be quite primitive if the child's behavior is to be changed. Philosophical and pseudo-ethical concerns regarding these artificial reinforcers, notably notions of "bribery" of children, may have to be dealt with directly. In view of the prognosis (O'Neal and Robins, 1958; Weiss, Minde, Werry, Douglas and Nemeth, 1971) of disruptive children, one can easily justify such benign, although educationally unconventional, means to produce effective social and academic behaviors, provided, of course, they *are* effective. The use of these back-up reinforcers is often only temporarily necessary. With time and proper chaining of social reinforcers with the more primitive reinforcers, the back-up reinforcers can be eliminated entirely. In addition, once skills are mastered, the reinforcers are usually able to be phased out.

As classroom enrollment increases, the likelihood of having moderately and severely handicapped children included should decrease; therefore, the need for employing tangible extrinsic reinforcers is lessened. The teacher who wishes to apply behavior modification technicques in his classroom will minimize this procedure's disadvantages if he utilizes natural reinforcers first. It is only when the natural reinforcers prove to be ineffective that token programs using tangible extrinsic reinforcers should temporarily be used. Once classroom behavior has improved, the back-up reinforcers should be withdrawn as soon as possible, through chaining of social reinforcers with the tangible reinforcers. Many times teachers persist in using extrinsic reinforcers because they overlook or minimize the potential reinforcement value of such obvious, naturalistic consequences as free time, art activities, extra recess time, serving as classroom monitor or tutor, and other individualized high-probability behaviors. For a wealth of additional suggestions on naturalistic classroom reinforcers, I recommend La Mancusa's entertaining *We Do Not Throw Rocks at the Teacher*.

None of the above problems is insurmountable. Their existence and likely appearance simply need to be recognized so that their efforts do not result in the abandonment of an otherwise effective intervention effort. Human variability is great; no method is likely to be equally effective for all children in all settings. At this juncture in the development of the field, the accumulating data of investigators (see O'Leary and Drabman) have convinced us that the utilization of techniques developed from the principles of reinforcement theory are the best available for the education of both the "atypical" and "normal" child in the public school setting. Further research in the application of these techniques in a variety of in-school settings can promise a hierarchy of effective intervention strategies keyed to the severity and persistence of an individual child's deviant behavior.

A major criticism of behavior modification in the past has been that it is limited to clinic or one-to-one situations; however, recent years have seen the extension of applying behavioral modification techniques from the clinic to the classroom, and from the individual to the entire group. Since its application to groups or the entire classroom has the greatest relevance for educators, a few recent studies will be cited.

Several projects have described token or social reinforcement systems used with a group within the classroom. Other investigators have utilized a reinforcer intrinsic to every class, i.e., teacher attention (Becker, et al., 1967). Barrish, Saunders and Wolf (1969) investigated the effects of a classroom behavior management technique based on natural classroom reinforcers other than teacher attention. The technique successfully utilized group competition for privileges in an effort to reduce disruptive class behavior.

Using behavior modification with the entire class, McKenzie and his associates (1968) relied on naturalistic class events for reinforcers. However, when the children's academic behaviors failed to reach an optimal level, their parents agreed to supply the children's allowances contingent upon their weekly grades. Significant increases in the children's academic behavior were reported. The inherent advantages of McKenzie's approach would certainly appear to merit additional investigation. By utilizing weekly allowances as back-up reinforcers, the teachers would not be required to spend undue additional time implementing the token system.

Successful reports of academic or behavioral gains in the often overlooked areas of junior and senior high schools were made by McAllister, et al. (1969), Nolen, Kunzelman and Haring (1967), and Broden and his associates (1970). McAllister and his associates demonstrated that the combination of disapproval for inappropriate talking and turning around, and praise for appropriate, incompatible behaviors substantially reduced the incidence of the target behaviors in a class of twenty-five students.

The following action research by Junod illustrates when an expected positive reinforcement may actually be a negative reinforcement under certain circumstances. In this study, gang recognition represented the preferred reinforcement which far surpassed other possible reinforcers. It is particularly important for the teacher to be aware of the significance of an adolescent's peers. For an interesting example of the power of gang membership upon its members, see Polsky's *Cottage Six* (1962).

An Educational Intervention for Socially Maladjusted Adolescents

by

Richard J. Junod

Aim. The object of this study was to reduce the number of inter-gang conflicts in the classroom and to generate social conformity among antagonistic gang members by pairing the influence of the gang with socialized inforcers.

Definition of Problem. An inter-gang conflict was defined as any stimulus initiated by a gang member that elicits an aversive reaction from one or more antipodal gang members and calls the attention of other students to the problem.

Subjects. The students of this study were unsentenced male adolescents awaiting trial at the House of Correction, aged sixteen to eighteen. Fifty-seven in all participated and mean class attendance was thirteen. All but six students were gang members.

Procedure. Baseline was collected for five sessions, each consisting of three and a half hours of observation time. The time element in the following treatments remains consistent with baseline. Treatment number one was based on a permissive, laizze-faire attitude taken by the teacher. The only time the teacher intervened was when a physical encounter was imminent. Treatment number two consisted of a "traditional approach" in handling conduct problems. Whenever an inter-gang conflict would arise, the teacher would embark on a tirade about the stupidity of belonging to a gang. Typical appeals and threats were made, such as "open your mouth one more time and you won't see a *point* (there already existed a behavior modification strategy whereby students earned points) for a month." Under Treatment number three the gang was presented as a positive entity and membership was premised on *total* allegiance, not only physical but also intellectual. Students were given the option of winning for themselves, hence the gang, Certificates of Excellence. Certificates displayed prominently the student's gang affiliation and bore the signature of the institution's warden. Thus social recognition for the gang and its single members was contingent upon academic excellence and a positive behavioral commitment.

Results and Discussion. Treatment number one terminated after the third session when it was felt that the permissive approach actually encouraged misbehaviors that almost tripled in three sessions. Treatment number two was equally ineffective in decreasing inter-gang conflicts. Negative comments made by the teacher were more than enough to not only encourage aversive behaviors among students, but also to generate overt hostility between teacher and students. Disintegration of classroom management, disorganization, frustration and increasing student resentment led to the abandonment of Treatment number two after the fifth session. Treatment number three was significantly more productive. Providing for recognition of the gang and utilizing the spirit of competition inherent in gang members proved to be effective reinforcers in attenuating inter-gang conflicts in the classroom. As more students became attracted to earning Certificates of Excellence, the frequency of the unwanted behaviors decreased. When high tallies occurred on the twelfth and twenty-sixth of March, they were not without explanation. A riot on the homicide wing on the eleventh precipitated hostile discussion on the twelfth, and two new students, in class three days, instigated a fight on the twenty-sixth.

Implications for Education. Behavior modification as an educational intervention seems to be quite effective in working with socially maladjusted youths, which comprise a group which Dunn claims is the most resistant to educational manipulation. The problem of peer recognition in lieu of social recognition by conduct problem students can be handled and controlled. Social reward can be employed as control for self improvement, once meaningful social contingencies are located and defined. The utilization of an "asocial entity" or of "sub-cultural influences" can effect education goals which otherwise would be unobtainable.

Generalization

The question of generalization of behavior is especially important in the area of special education, since the special child may move through trials in the regular class with part-time placement in a resource room or a special class with a behavioral orientation. An example of the problem is seen in the following study.

Behavior-problem children who attended a resource room for one or two periods a day (Glavin, Quay, Annesley, and Werry, 1971) made significant improvement academically and behaviorally while in the resource room. Children were scheduled in the resource room for the period in the day during which their teacher said they were functioning least effectively in the regular class. Since the majority were also performing below expected grade level academically, the program emphasized academic remediation with the use of extrinsic reinforcement contingencies. Further examination of the data revealed that while the experimental group increased its attending behavior while in the resource room, attention in the regular classroom did not improve, nor did it differ from the controls.

The data on attending behavior provided another demonstration of the need to program generalization: conditions in the regular class must clearly be changed to support behavior learned in the resource room. It is not at all likely that such changes can be brought about by limited contact between resource room staff and the regular class teachers which occurred during the course of our implementation of the resource room model. Since there is little research evidence that generalization of behavior will occur fortuitously after utilizing a token program with extrinsic back-up reinforcers, the following suggestions are offered for achieving generalization.

1. Replace extrinsic reinforcers as quickly as possible and maintain the newly developed behavior with social reinforcers, natural reinforcers and student-administered contingency contracts.
2. Stress reinforcing academic rather than behavioral change. The successful completion of an academic goal is almost always incompatible with seriously disruptive behavior in the classroom, while reinforcing appropriate behavior does not necessarily lead to improved academic gains. In addition, if the child is unable to compete academically upon his return to the regular classroom, the disruptive behavior is likely to emerge again.
3. Realize that the regular class teacher should be assisted in individualizing the child's curriculum and in maintaining appropriate management techniques when the child is to be phased back to the regular class.
4. Teach the students to collect and evaluate their own behavioral data.
5. Teach the children contingency contracting, moving from teacher-directed goals to mutually-directed targets, and finally to student-initiated goals and contingencies when possible.

Conclusion

The results of these studies suggest an increased likelihood of adoption of behavior modification techniques by the classroom teacher. Our experience has shown that undergraduate and graduate students can quickly and successfully implement these techniques in action research projects as part of a course's requirements. To insure continued use of the techniques once the student has completed his training, it is suggested that data collection techniques be as simple as possible and that naturalistic reinforcers found in the school situation be utilized whenever possible to minimize expense. Data collection and even analysis can often be left to the pupils, particularly under a contingency contracting situation. Supervising a contingency managed classroom is always easier when the teacher can acquire the aid of another person. Teacher aids, parents or other school personnel are often suggested but are frequently not available. However, student aids from the class itself may serve many useful functions, such as class monitors of behavior, recorders or correctors of work assignments, and sometimes even academic remedial helpers. Teachers choosing academic target goals (which is encouraged) frequently report unexpected concomitant behavioral gains. Finally, I strongly urge the beginning practitioner of behavior modification techniques to seek competent supervisory support, especially if he contemplates initiating a token program using the more powerful but complicated extrinsic reinforcers.

References

Baer, D. M., M. M. Wolf and T. R. Risley. "Some current dimensions of applied behavior analysis." *Journal of Applied Behavior Analysis* (1968), *1*, 91–97.

Barrish, H.H., M. Saunders and M. M. Wolf. "Good behavior game: Effects of individual contingencies for group consequences on disruptive behavior in a classroom." *Journal of Applied Behavior Analysis* (1969), *1*, 287–307.

Becker, W.C., C. H. Madsen, Jr., C. R. Arnold and D. R. Thomas. "The contingent use of teacher attention and praise in reducing classroom behavior problems." *Journal of Special Education* (1967), *1*, 287–308.

Broden, M., R. V. Hall, A. Dunlap, and R. Clark. "Effects of teacher attention and a token reinforcement system in a junior high school special education class." *Exceptional Children* (1970), *36*, 341–49.

Glavin, J. P., H. C. Quay, F. R. Annesley and J. S. Werry. "An experimental resource room program for classroom behavior problem children." *Exceptional Children* (1971), *38*, 131–37.

Glavin, J. P., H. C. Quay and J. S. Werry. "Behavioral and academic gains of conduct problem children in different classroom settings." *Exceptional Children* (1971), *37*, 441–46.

La Mancusa, K. *We Do Not Throw Rocks at the Teacher*. Scranton, Pa.: International Textbooks Co., 1966.

MacMillan, D. L. and S. R. Forness. "Behavior modification: Limitations and liabilities." *Exceptional Children* (1970) *37*, 291–97.

Maer, M. L. "Some limitation of the application of reinforcement theory to education." *School and Society* (1968), *96*, (2303), 108–110.

McAllister, L.W., J. G. Stachowiak, D. W. Baer and L. Conderman. "The application of operant conditioning techniques in a secondary school classroom." *Journal of Applied Behavior Analysis* (1969), *2*, 277–285.

McKenzie, H.S., M. Clark, M. M. Wolf, R. Kothera and C. Benson. "Behavior modifications of children with learning disabilities using grades as tokens and allowances as back-up reinforcers." *Exceptional Children* (1968), *34*, 163–68.

Nolen, P. A., H. P. Kunzelman and N. G. Haring. "Behavioral modification in a junior high learning disabilities classroom." *Exceptional Children* (1967), *34*, 163–68.

O'Leary, K.D. and R. Drabman. "Token reinforcement programs in the classroom: A review." *Psychological Bulletin* (1971), *75*, 379–98.

O'Neal, P. and L. N. Robins."The relation of childhood behavior problems to adult psychiatric status: A thirty-year follow-up study of 150 subjects." *American Journal of Psychiatry* (1958), *114*, 961–69.

Quay, H. C., R. L. Sprague, J. S. Werry, and M. M. McQueen. "Conditioning visual orientation of conduct problem children in the classroom." *Journal of Experimental Child Psychology* (1967), *5*, 512–17.

Staats, A. W. *Child Learning, Intelligence and Personality: Principles of a Behavioral Interaction Approach*. New York: Harper and Row, 1971.

Weiss, G., K. Minde, J. Werry, V. Douglas and E. Nemeth. "Studies on the hyperactive child VIII. Five year follow-up." *Archives of General Psychiatry*. (1971), *24* (5), 409–414.

Section 2

Different Types of Reinforcement Procedures and Teaching Strategies

5

Modeling and Vicarious Reinforcement

The procedures discussed in this chapter have been given the names modeling and vicarious reinforcement. Modeling refers to the probability of a child's response changing as a consequence of his having observed a model exhibit the same or similar behavior with consequences *directly* affecting the child. With vicarious reinforcement, the consequences *indirectly* impinge upon the child through his observation of the direct consequences of another child's behavior.

Examples of modeling are often seen in young children's play activities. Indeed, if a teacher wishes an accurate reenactment of how he carries out his teaching role, he need only suggest that his class play "school" with different pupils playing the teacher. This particular learning experience befell me as a beginning teacher of twenty-two mentally retarded boys. In a moment of pique at the children's lack of cooperation, I suggested they teach themselves by taking turns being teacher. The outcome was traumatic but informative, and I continued to use this method occasionally in subsequent years of teaching as a check on my behavior.

Modeling Procedures Versus Operant Conditioning

In our discussion of operant conditioning and positive reinforcement, one serious problem was mentioned: how to make the child initiate the response in the first place. If a response does not exist in the child's repertoire, then it cannot be reinforced. If the behavior to be learned is complex, then it must be broken down into its component elements, and shaping of successive approximations toward the desired goal must be utilized. Thus, relying solely upon positive reinforcement may be useful in maintaining behavior that already exists, but it is often slow and inefficient in developing new behaviors. Modeling may represent a more effective means than positive reinforcement of establishing new response patterns.

A behavior pattern, once acquired through modeling, is often maintained without deliberate external reinforcements. This point is of crucial importance when one considers the still questionable utility of positive reinforcement on the generalization and permanence of newly acquired behavior. While both generalization and permanance of behavior have been effected using operant methods in laboratory settings, the results in applying these methods in the classroom are still unsubstantiated. In contrast, the modeling procedure provides evidence of permanence. In a follow-up investigation, Thelen (1970) found that children's modeled self-derogations continued after several months without subsequent modeling experiences. Bandura, Blanchard and Ritter (1968) reported sustained changes after one month in attitudes, behavior and emotional responsiveness. The generalization of modeling effects was demonstrated by Bandura and McDonald (1963) and Bandura and Mischel (1965) when their subjects' responses were consistent under varying stimulus conditions and with the model no longer present.

Effects of Modeling on Children's Behavior

The studies reviewed in this chapter report that modeling is effective in changing a wide range of behavior. However, as O'Leary and O'Leary (1972) point out, theorists do not agree on the outcome of modeling. For example, psychoanalytic theory suggests that when children view violence, the catharsis hypothesis indicates that viewing aggressive actions will satisfy violent impulses and thus reduce the possibility of overt aggression. In contrast, Bandura, Ross and Ross (1963) have reported that controlled experimental research indicates the opposite: when children observe violence, they are more likely to act aggressively themselves.

Although theoretical disputes still remain, all seem to agree that the modeling effect does take place. Sarason and Ganzer (1969) and Sarason (1968) made major studies using the modeling paradigm with conduct-problem adolescent delinquents. Their procedure involved models dramatizing scripts where acceptable patterns of social behavior were shown. Afterward, the juvenile delinquents would rehearse the scene. Group discussion and role playing were also used. Both staff and delinquents reported increased prosocial behaviors.

Gittelman (1965) utilized role rehersal to change aggressive behavior in older children. The children were asked to describe situations that caused hostility in them, and these incidents were arranged in a hierarchy from least to most intensity. Then the situations were rehearsed sequentially starting with the least intense incidents to help the children to cope with them in a more acceptable manner.

This brief review of research using modeling has concentrated on changing aggressive behavior in children, but in the case of humans a wide variety of other behavior patterns have been altered through modeling procedures. Perhaps of greatest interest to the reader, among the diverse classes of behavior that have been developed, are the studies which have dealt with teaching styles. Fesbach (1967) reported that imitative behavior varied with children of differing personality characteristics and social background depending upon differences in teachers' reinforcement style. McDonald and Allen (1967) reported on the training effects on teachers' performance of feedback and modeling procedure.

Factors Controlling the Modeling Effect

It is well known that students most readily identify with school sports heroes and older students. However, Flanders (1968) reported a number of characteristics of the observer which influence the degree of his imitative behavior. These factors include: race, sex, socioeconomic level, and personality characteristics. For example, dependent children are found to be more likely to model the behavior of others. Altman and Talkington (1971) have elaborated upon the significance of this finding by suggesting that the high suggestibility characteristic of the mentally retarded may be due to their being outer-rather than inner-directed. The outer-directed person is attributed with a reliance on external clues for his action, as a function of frequent past failure experiences. The authors thus hypothesize that heightened dependency on outside stimuli should make the retarded child more susceptible to the modeling effect.

The ability of a child to model appears to be a function of several variables. A child must be able to attend to the model's behavior. This proved to be an initial difficulty for Lovaas (1968) who developed a comprehensive program of speech therapy with schizophrenic children involving modeling procedures. Also, the complexity of the stimuli must be considered. Lovaas found it necessary to identify each element in the response to be modeled, place them in a hierarchy, and present the least difficult ones first. Thus it is necessary to know both the developmental level of the learner and the components of the behavior one wishes to have modeled.

Bronfenbrenner (1970) reported that the characteristics of the model include such things as:

> The extent to which the teacher is perceived as possessing a high degree of competence, status, and control over resources.
> The extent to which the teacher has been perceived as nurturant and supportive in the past.
> The most contagious models are apt to be those who are major sources of support and control in his surroundings, namely his parents, playmates and older children, and adults who play a prominent role in his everyday life.
> The degree to which the student perceives the model as similar to himself.
> The use of several models exhibiting similar behavior is more effective in changing behavior than the use of a single model.
> The extent to which a model's behavior is a salient feature in the actions of a group to which the child already belongs or aspires to be a member.

Bronfenbrenner suggests that the teacher should not only serve as a model but should actively seek out other appropriate models in the classroom. These findings should suggest many ramifications to the teacher regarding peer teaching, social reinforcement and contingency management, and the teacher's own adopted role in the classroom.

The student's motivation should also be ensured while the modeling tasks are being performed. Lovaas found it necessary to consistently reinforce each imitative verbal response of the schizophrenic child while simultaneously withholding reinforcement when the child inappropriately verbalized. Thus, with severely handicapped children, selective reinforcement of each appropriate response is highly effective. Bandura (1969) reports that the consequences of the modeled behavior are very important in determining the extent of imitation. On the other hand, Bandura (1965) says that reinforcement may not always be of serious concern in the utilization of modeling techniques, in that social models acquired responses with no reinforcements dispensed to either the models or the observers.

Strategy for Employing Modeling

Earlier in this chapter it was mentioned that modeling can promote behavior not previously in the persons repertoire, as well as modify misbehavior. While new behavior patterns can emerge solely through the modeling effect, behavioral change can be facilitated by providing successive approximations to the desired goal, and by giving positive reinforcement for each successful approximation. The major point in this strategy is to identify each successive approximation in the behavioral hierarchy, beginning with the least anxiety-arousing one. The model demonstrates each step, one by one, to the child. The child must successfully imitate each step before moving to the next hardest approximation. If anxiety is shown, the child should be asked to repeat the last previously successful step. If the child remains anxious, the hierarchy should be reexamined for possible error. Once the child is successful at the new approximation he should be immediately reinforced. Only a few approximations should be modeled at one time, and the schedule of reinforcement should be gradually diminished. If the teacher is attempting to change behavior that occurs outside the classroom, such as in the gym, hallway or lunchroom, he must then switch to the natural setting and reinforce the child in the presence of the gym instructor, etc., and those people in the natural setting should be instructed on how to reinforce and maintain the child's new behavior.

The following strategy was employed by one of the author's students in an introductory course on teaching behavior-disordered children. The course content included a few readings and three or four class lectures and discussions on applying some rudimentary behavioral techniques. The students were encouraged to discuss each step of their action research project in small group discussions as well as with their instructor. Diane Bryen's project successfully incorporated many of the steps recommended for applying the modeling technique.

Developing Sound-Changing into Words in a Five-Year-Old Mongoloid Girl

by

Diane Bryen

The object of this study was to begin language training in a young mongoloid child. The experimenter (E) initiated this behavior modification program because after two months of language training, only five words had been crudely learned. Work similar to this study has been done using operant procedures in speech and language training.

Subject. The subject (S) of this study was a five-year-old Negro girl. S had been seen and diagnosed by Children's Hospital of Philadelphia. The diagnosis stated that S was a mongoloid child, with moderate to severe retardation. More exact findings had not been obtained because the child lacked language and sufficient attention and impulse control to be adequately tested. S was in good health, except for poor vision and a slight heart murmur.

The subject's family was intact, with mother and father living at home with five other siblings. The parents accepted the child's incompetencies, and placed much focus on her strengths. Their main concern was her lack of speech, although the child was able to get needs and wishes fulfilled by gesturing and pulling people to what she wanted. Thus, there had been little need for the child to develop speech.

Both mother and father had been involved in previous treatment with the child. They had had an active part in implementing various perceptual-motor training methods under the supervision of the experimenter.

Procedure. The behavior which E was to modify was to increase the number of nouns the subject emitted in imitation. The child had no language skills except for the use of the expressions "No!" and "Shut up!" The experimenter collected baseline data in the kitchen of the subject's home. This data period took three weeks, with two twenty-minute sessions each week. The total number of days E spent collecting baseline data was six. Total minutes spent were 120. S was seated on a high chair at the kitchen table. E sat facing her, at the table. E would say, "Say mama," and if the child was able to come close to imitation, this would count as one noun spoken. No response by E was made after S's response. The subject was quite distractable during this time.

On the fourth week, treatment number one began. Food was used as the primary reinforcement. The mother did not feed S that day, depriving the child of all food. S had quite an appetite, thus she was exceedingly hungry by 1:00 p.m., when E arrived. S sat in her high chair with E facing her. A screen was placed behind E and S, eliminating much extraneous stimuli. Nothing was on the table but a bowl of cereal and milk and a spoon. E would say, "Say mama," and if the child imitated the sound at all, a small teaspoon of cereal was placed in her mouth, and E would say "good," or "that's right." At first any verbal response was rewarded, then each response had to closer approximate the given word.

By the end of the fourth twenty-minute session of treatment (fifth week), ten nouns were emitted in imitation. These words were still very crude and it was quite apparent that S lacked the ability to produce many of the needed speech sounds.

During the sixth week, treatment number two began. E began by having the child learn to imitate specific speech sounds. Modifying the environment somewhat more, E decided to use a discriminating stimulus. A red apron was worn by E and a red smock was worn by S during each twenty-minute session. The mother also became an active member of the treatment program. She observed from behind the screen during the treatment session and she continued the treatment during the time E was not present. The mother kept excellent records of speech sounds emitted by S. In one week, six twenty-minute sessions, S had adequately learned all speech sounds.

The next phase of treatment involved chaining sounds into words. E would say, "Say ma." Then E would say, "Say mama." By the eighth week (the third week of treatment number two), the mother became the experimenter, with E observing from behind the screen. Also the use of intermittant reinforcement (fixed interval) began.

Results and Plans for the Future. The subject's use of nouns (by chaining sounds in imitation) increased to twenty. The mother, under supervision by E, became quite skilled.

E and the mother are continuing to use operant conditioning procedures. The next step is to use objects and pictures of objects with the auditory stimulus. After this has been accomplished, the auditory stimulus will be faded and only the object or picture will be presented with the question, "What is this?"

The parents are beginning to rely more upon verbal responses from S, instead of gestures. It is a long procedure, because the child's repertoire continues to be quite limited. However, the parents are continually amazed at the "rapid" progress being made.

Vicarious Reinforcement

In the classroom, a child's peers often see his behavior rewarded or punished. Bandura (1969) has shown that the rewarding or punishing of one student can have a powerful effect upon his classmates to perform the same behavior. Many primary-grade teachers have achieved successful classroom management by unwittingly applying this principle of rewarding individual students in front of the whole class. Statements such as "Look how hard Joe is working" can produce a horde of hard working first-graders.

Several factors influence the amount of impact this technique has. The extent to which vicarious learning will occur depends upon the same factors as did modeling, that is age, sex, socioeconomic status, race, and intellectual status. If the student has much prestige or status with his classmates, then the effect will be enhanced. Bandura suggests that the teacher who can control the leaders of the class will have a much easier time controlling the entire class. Kounin (1970) indicates that the orientation (task-focus versus approval-focus) affects the amount of imitation by the child's peers. The use of task-focused techniques increased students' estimates of the teacher's skill more than did witnessesing approval-focused methods. In addition, students who viewed task-focused techniques increased their interest in the subject matter more than students who observed approval-focused methods.

Conclusion

Many old-time teachers and even some present-day students in teacher-training programs have completed their training with the only advice given on classroom management being: "Be firm, fair and consistent." The author feels that while this is certainly an inappropriate amount of preparation for a future teacher, the advice is still commendable in terms of the principle of vicarious reinforcement. Teacher firmness is important, especially in handling acting-out or conduct-problem children, because it not only reduces the deviancy of the individual child, but also that of his classmates. Once the class rules have been established, it is imperative that the teacher be consistent. When the class sees that a misbehaving child is not admonished, the likelihood is that the teacher will lose control of the class. Finally, the teacher must be fair. If the teacher substitutes an overbearing or dictatorial approach for a fair one, it is likely to increase disruptive behavior among the entire class as well as the individual offender.

Since modeling can be such a powerful and pervasive behavioral technique, the factors controlling its effect should certainly suggest that the teacher not be punitive or dictatorial; nor should he attempt to become "one of the boys"—a pal rather than a teacher. Modeling and vicarious reinforcement are two of the most overlooked of all behavioral techniques in terms of study and application of them in teacher training and classroom management. However, they appear to hold great relevancy and promise for the future.

References

Altman, R. and L. Talkington. "Modeling: an alternative behavior modification approach for retardates." *Mental Retardation* (1971), *9*, 20–23.

Bandura, A. "Influence of models' reinforcement contingencies on the acquisition of imitative responses." *Journal of Personality and Social Psychology* (1965), 589–95.

_____. *Principles of Behavior Modification.* New York: Holt, Rinehart and Winston, 1969.

Bandura, A., E. D. Blanchard, and B. J. Ritter. "The relative efficacy of desensitization and modeling therapeutic approaches for inducing behavioral, affective and attitudinal changes." Unpublished manuscript. Stanford University, 1968.

Bandura, A., and F. J. McDonald. "The influence of social reinforcement and the behavior of models in shaping children's moral judgments." *Journal of Abnormal and Social Psychology* 1963, *67*, 274–81.

Bandura, A., and W. Mischel. "The influence of models in modifying delay of gratification patterns." *Journal of Personality and Social Psychology* (1965), *2*, 698–705.

Bandura, A., D. Ross and S. A. Ross. Imitation of film-mediated aggressive models. *Journal of Abnormal and Social Psychology* (1963), *66*, 3–11.

Benton, A. "Effects of the timing of negative response consequences on the observational learning of resistance to temptation in children." *Dissertation Abstracts* (1967), *27*, 2153–2154.

Bronfenbrenner, U. *Two Worlds of Childhood. U. S. and U.S.S.R.* New York: Russell Sage Foundation, 1970.

Fesbach, N. D. "Variations in teachers' reinforcement style and imitative behavior of children differing in personality characteristics and social background." Unpublished manuscript. University of California, Los Angeles, 1967.

Flanders, J. "A reviewof research on imitative behavior." *Psychological Bulletin* (1968), *69* (5), 316–37.

Gittleman, M. "Behavioral rehearsal as a technique in child treatment." *Journal of Child Psychology and Psychiatry* (1965), *6*, 251–55.

Kounin, J. *Discipline and Group Management in Classrooms.* New York: Holt, Rinehart and Winston, Inc., 1970.

Lovaas, O. I. "Somestudies on the treatment of childhood schizophrenia." In J. Schlein (ed.), *Research in Psychotherapy.* Washington, D.C.: American Psychological Association, 1968, 103–21.

McDonald, F. and D. W. Allen. "Training effects of feedback and modeling procedures on teaching performance." Unpublished manuscript. Stanford University, 1967.

O'Leary, K. D. and S. O'Leary.*Classroom Management: The Successful Use of Behavior Modification.* New York: Pergamon Press, Inc. 1972.

Sarason, I. G. "Verbal learning, modeling, and juvenile delinquency." *American Psychologist* (1968), *23*, 254–66.

Sarason, I. G. and V. J. Ganzer. "Developing appropriate social behaviors of juvenile delinquents." In J. Krumboltz and C. Thorensen (eds.), *Behavioral Counseling: Cases and Techniques*. New York: Holt, Rinehart and Winston, 1969. 216–37.

Thelen, M. H. "Long-term retention of verbal imitation." *Developmental Psychology* (1970), *3*, 29–31.

Walters, R., R. Parke and V. Cane. "Timing of punishment and the observation of consequences to others as determinants of response inhibition." *Journal of Experimental Child Psychology* (1965), *2*, 10–30.

Zigler, E. "Mental retardation: Current issues and approaches." In L. W. Hoffman and M. L. Hoffman (eds.), *Review of child development research*, Vol. 2. New York: Russell Sage Foundation, 1966.

6

Social Reinforcement

Many teachers encounter discipline problems as one of the biggest detriments to effective teaching. Too much time is spent getting the class ready to learn, resulting in too little time for teaching the lesson. The purpose of this chapter is to demonstrate how positive social reinforcement can reduce disruptive behavior in a normal classroom without the behavior modification program becoming a very complicated and tedious chore for the teacher. There are two main categories of reinforcement: social incentives (being praised or reprimanded, attended to or ignored by the teacher), and secondary reinforcers (tokens to be traded in for goods or privileges). This chapter responds to the question: *which rewards are more useful, practical and effective.*

For our purposes social behavior may be defined as behavior of the student which is being or has been influenced by other people in his environment. From the time a person is born, he is constantly being reinforced socially by his parents, his friends, and teachers. Social reinforcement plays an important role in the development of the personality of the human organism. It is this reinforcement which will determine his knowledge of both right and wrong, and which will shape his normal characteristics. If a child is constantly given negative social reinforcements, this will be reflected in his attitudes toward others and in his ability to adjust to the various situations in which he will become involved in later life. It is very important for the parent to stress the proper reinforcement for the appropriate situation.

Social reinforcements develop in various stages. They come first from the parents during the early years of the child's life. The second stage is reinforcement from his peers, which usually begins during the later stages of early childhood. The final stage occurs when the child enters school. This period now includes reinforcement from both adults (his teachers), and peers (his fellow students). It is during this period, when reinforcement can occur from two different sources at the same time, that the child must decide which is more important—the social reinforcement from his teacher or the welcome support of his peers. An effective method of dealing with maladaptive behavior is a program that would combine both types of reinforcement.

Praising appropriate student behavior is probably the most underestimated method for controlling classroom behavior even though it has been widely studied. In study after study, results show that a teacher can manipulate student behavior by displaying approval for appropriate behavior. However, a practical method for utilizing this principle is often ignored in day-to-day classroom situations. In addition, the teacher should not underestimate the skill required for utilizing praise effectively.

Studies on Social Incentives

The role of verbal incentives in learning has been considered in many studies. The most widely studied verbal incentive has been teacher praise. Most studies have confirmed that teacher praise tends to facilitate learning. Praise, however, is not the only form of social incentive. Being reproved or ignored by the teacher are also forms of incentives. Reproof has been shown to have a debilitating effect in the classroom. Being ignored by the teacher for inappropriate behavior has been shown to be effective if it is combined with praise for appropriate behavior. Madsen, Becker and Thomas (1968) conducted a study in which they varied the behavior of two elementary school teachers. It was an attempt to determine the effects on classroom behavior of: rules, ignoring inappropriate behavior, and showing approval for appropriate behavior. Following baseline recordings, rules, ignoring and approval conditions were introduced one at a time. Their conclusions were: rules alone exerted little effect on classroom behavior; ignoring inappropriate behavior and showing approval for appropriate behavior (in combination) were very effective in achieving better classroom behavior; and showing approval for appropriate behavior is probably the key to effective classroom management. Another study was carried out by Becker, et al. (1968), in which he also studied the effects of teacher behavior (social reinforcement) on classroom behavior. His results showed that approving responses from the teacher served as a positive reinforcer in maintaining appropriate classroom behavior.

Both of these studies demonstrate that teacher approval for appropriate behavior has great potential as a reinforcer. The approving behaviors used in the two studies were: reassuring comments ("you're doing a fine job"), smiles, and contact (a pat on the back or placing a hand on the shoulder). Disapproval of inappropriate behavior (reprimanding the pupil) has been repeatedly shown to be ineffective. It has made behavior worse in some cases. The theory behind the use of social incentives can clarify why punishment or aversive incentives do not work. Stated simply: *children seek approval and support from adults.* Theoretically, then, when children are praised for appropriate behavior and ignored when they misbehave, they will continue activities that earn teachers' praise. In other words, they will spend most of their time behaving and performing appropriately. On the other hand, when praise is inconsistent, and reproof and disapproval are being used, the classroom will take on an atmosphere of hostility.

O'Leary and Becker (1969) explain that the teacher who continually reprimands will condition undesirable emotional responses in the student. Also, disapproval of undesirable behavior tells the child that a certain behavior is inappropriate but does not signify what is appropriate. Hence the child will experiment to find appropriate actions. While doing this he will probably go through a whole gamut of inappropriate behavior. Children who have experienced generalized negative emotional conditioning are difficult with others. Teachers are at the mercy of the strong effects of this emotional conditioning. O'Leary and Becker found that praising for appropriate behavior combined with ignoring inappropriate behavior reduced the average time of disruptive behavior fifty-four to thirty-two percent. However, when reprimands for inappropriate behavior were introduced, the disruptive behavior time rose again to the baseline level.

Another important aspect of positive social reinforcement is the frequency of its use. Especially during the initial stages of the use of social incentives, the frequency of teacher praise is very important. In the beginning teachers should try to praise as many appropriate behaviors as possible. Even when the procedure has been in progress for a while, frequent praise has been shown to be effective. Clark and Walberg (1969) found that the frequency of praise was indeed an important factor. In their study two groups of children were used. One group was praised at a level normally used in the classroom. The second group was given extra praise whenever possible. The target was spelling. After four weeks a post-test showed that the normal praise group gained seven to eight words spelled correctly. The high praise group gained an average of sixteen words.

Teachers should carefully consider behaviors to be praised as to their compatability with classroom learning. The probability that Johnny will continue to call out in class when no attention is given him is very slim if he receives frequent attention for raising his hand before he speaks. Johnny cannot be raising his hand to answer and not raising his hand at the same time; these are incompatible behaviors. Nor can he be sitting at his seat quiely and jumping impatiently out of his desk simultaneously. If Johnny is praised for raising his hand and ignored for calling out, it is logical to assume that he will raise his hand more frequently and call out less. A simple rule for reducing disruptive classroom behavior is: Increase through positive social reinforcement appropriate behaviors which are incompatible with behaviors to be eliminated, and when possible, decrease the inappropriate behaviors by ignoring them.

Although this may seem little more than common sense, various scientific procedures must be observed. In successfully utilizing operant conditioning techniques, the behavior to be changed must be observable and countable. The consequences must be contingent. In other words, the behavior should be a function of the nature of the consequence, that is, either favorable or unfavorable. If one were to observe teacher-pupil interaction in an unruly classroom, many inconsistencies would be evident between behavior and its consequences. If the situation were to be replaced by a systematic approach to problem behavior through reinforcement procedures, the same classroom could be controlled. In a study by Thomas, Becker and Armstrong (1971), disruptive behavior was first produced and then removed in a class of twenty-eight public school children who were normally well-behaved. The children's behavior (good or bad) was manipulated by the teacher's responses (approving or disapproving).

The remainder of this chapter will deal specifically with two types of incentives: teacher reinforcement and peer reinforcement. The individual will be dealt with in the discussion of teacher reinforcement, while the use of the group will be discussed in the section on peer reinforcement.

The Teacher as Social Reinforcer

One of the most important aspects of any classroom is the management of behavior. One of the basic methods of correcting maladaptive behavior is through the use of reinforcements applied by the teacher. A most important reinforcer on the part of the teacher is his own behavior, especially his personality. In their early school years children tend to be imitators of the behavior of older people. They will tend to imitate the way the teacher responds to various situations. A teacher who lacks confidence in himself will not generally create a classroom situation that resounds with confidence. Teachers can create maladaptive behavior; they do not have to rely on their students to create it. They can do this by the lack of explicit classroom rules.

Maladaptive behavior can also be corrected by them through the use of verbal reinforcements. These reinforcements can be positive or negative depending upon the behavior. According to a study conducted by Becker, et al. (1968), ignoring disruptive behavior is a major element of modifying that behavior. Attention to the maladaptive behavior may serve to strengthen or reinforce what you are trying to correct. Behavior may be strengthened by paying attention to it, even though the teacher may think that he is punishing that behavior. The child may relish the attention that he is getting even if it is in the form of punishment. He may continue to practice the behavior in order to get attention.

One of the major rules that can be discovered from Becker's study is that praise should be varied and spread around. Becker also states that the teacher should tell the child why he is being praised. The study by Dickinson (1968) found that praise for appropriate behavior, and calm but firm reprimands are probably the most useful combination of social stimuli on the part of the teacher for maintaining appropriate behavior. Two things which the teacher must not practice are: verbal reprimands that are not backed up, and constant threats that are not carried through. These tend to lessen the effectiveness of both praise and reprimands.

Another method of social reinforcement that can be used by the teacher is touch. This could consist of a pat on the back, an embrace, or holding the child's hand. The study conducted by Becker, et al. (1968), also suggests such methods as kissing and allowing the child to sit on one's lap as useful methods of physical reinforcement by the teacher. Sometimes these two methods are frowned upon by the parents of the students, but physical reinforcement gives the child something that is both tangible and concrete. These reinforcements are not used as frequently as verbal reinforcements, mainly because the teacher can reach more students at one time through word of mouth. Physical reinforcements may be more effective with the individual student because they are on a more personal level than verbal reinforcements.

In summary, the teacher is a most important player in the game of classroom discipline. He must set the rules that govern his classroom and, in doing so, he will govern the behavior of each student.

The following example of action research by Walsh reports the results of positive social reinforcement by the teacher to decrease the instances of disruptive behavior in a sixth grade math class with twenty-five students.

Behavior Modification Techniques in a Normal Public School Classroom

by

Mary Ellen Walsh

It is the opinion of the teacher that on-task behavior is supported by an atmosphere in which the children can work free of distractions. Since this was not the case, the teacher designed to lessen the number of distractions, using praise as a social reinforcer to strengthen on-task nondisruptive behavior.

Problem. While the teacher worked with any of the three groups or while giving individualized instruction, the other students were assigned tasks to complete and to hand in at the end of each period. Many of the students would become very vocal as they worked on these tasks. Inappropriate calling out was defined as any audible vocalization that was deemed unnecessary or unnatural. Coughing, sneezing, belching or clearing the throat in an exaggerated manner were also included. The problem was not one caused by the difficulty of the work (an aide was there to assist) as much as it was one where the children expressed quite freely and braggadociously their delight with their successes. "See, I told you it was right" or "Hey, I did it!" can be overdone.

Situation. Data was collected for twenty consecutive days over a forty-minute period from 11:45 to 12:25 each day. The first ten days were used to establish baseline data with intervention beginning on day eleven and proceeding to day twenty. The data was collected by a cooperative student teacher during baseline who trained a student in the same procedure for the intervention period.

Procedure. The baseline data was collected under normal classroom conditions with "business going on as usual." No effort was made by the teacher to change her regular mode of operations. The baseline data was collected for ten consecutive days. The number of praise comments averaged around a midpoint of .3 per minute and an average of nineteen instances of calling-out behavior.

Social Reinforcement

Intervention began on day eleven and consisted of curtailing all negative reactions to this calling out behavior. Consistently, the teacher praised those children who were working on their assignments orally as well as through non-verbal communications suggesting the teacher's satisfaction with their on-task behavior. "Gee, you are working hard!" or a pat on the shoulder conveyed to the individual student as well as to the class that quiet on-task behavior would bring them the social approval of the teacher. When a child's calling out behavior became excessive, (successive outbursts over a two-minute period) the teacher or the aide would quietly approach the child and review the work that he had accomplished. At this time, the teacher or aide would positively encourage the child to proceed to keep working. "Let's see how many you can do without stopping. Take your time, but keep working." If, as was found in one instance, this attention was not working toward a decrease in calling out behavior, the teacher supported the child when he was quiet and ignored the child when he called out. In this one instance the social approval supported the behavior that we wished to change, therefore, the method of approval had to change.

The number of praise comments more than doubled to .89 per minute during intervention. Most important, the number of instances of calling out behavior averaged nineteen per forty-minute period and during the ten-day intervention period these instances decreased to an average of thirteen.

Evaluation. It appeared that there was a direct relationship between increased praise and the lessening of instances of calling out behavior. The type of praise as well as the number of praise comments was felt to be significant. While the teacher was establishing the baseline data, it was noticed that the majority of praise comments pertained to the quality of work produced and not specifically to the manner in which the children worked. Also, these comments usually pertained to the particular group with which the teacher was immediately working rather than to those groups working independently.

The number of instances of calling out behavior did lessen with the increased praise. They did so, however, in rise and fall patterns. It is the teacher's belief that if this study was continued, the pattern would stabilize with a lesser degree of rise and fall variance.

It was predictable and interesting that the greatest rise in calling out behavior during intervention exhibited itself on Fridays. Fridays certainly do have an adverse effect on children and teachers. All teachers await the application of behavioral techniques to cure the ills of Fridays!

The following are rules deducted from various studies concerning the use of verbal reinforcement by the teacher: The first is that the teacher should praise only on those occasions that warrant it, i.e., when the student behaves appropriately for the situation in which he is involved; praise should be varied and spread among the class; the teacher should tell the student why he is being praised; and finally, he should either praise appropriate behavior and ignore maladaptive behavior, or combine praise for appropriate behavior with calm but firm reprimands for misbehavior. Teachers who follow the rules that are mentioned above to set up an effective method of correcting maladaptive behavior within the classroom, should have few classroom management problems.

Peer Reinforcement and Pressure

A very important influence on the behavior of children in school is their classmates. This is especially true on the secondary level. His peers give the student social reinforcement just as his teacher does. One study conducted by Barrish, et al. (1969), established a game which depended upon the behavior of everyone in the classroom. A fourth grade class was divided into two teams. The goals that each team sought were privileges that are available in almost every classroom. Disruptive behavior on the part of any member of the team resulted in possible loss of privileges for every member of his team. The results of this study showed that the game had a reliable effect on correcting the maladaptive behavior occurring in the class; however, the principal and teacher both admitted that there was a classroom management problem involving two students who had been referred to the principal's office on several occasions for disruptive behavior. Both were on the same team and consistently gained a number of marks for their team. The authors came to the conclusion that the maladaptive behavior of these two was being reinforced by their peers through appreciative attention directed toward them. Pressure was applied to the misbehaving individuals by the peers, through the use of challenging stares and threatening glances when they misbehaved, and encouraging praise on the part of the other team members when they behaved appropriately.

A study by Schmidt (1969) dealt with the effects of peer pressure on a class of twenty-nine fourth grade students. They were selected because of excessive noise during free study periods. The rewards that were offered were an additional two minutes of gym period, and a two minute break after each ten minute period of unbroken quiet. Peer pressure was very intense and visible in the forms of threatening gestures, arm movement, and facial expressions being directed toward the more noisy members of the class. The results of this study again showed that while the teacher was applying social reinforcement in the forms of rewards and privileges, the students or peers were applying pressure on each other in order to receive them.

Several other studies dealt with the subject of peer pressure. Andrews

Social Reinforcement 75

(1971) concluded that the introduction of reinforcement involving the correct behavior of every class member brought about immense pressure on each student involved. The major source of pressure was exerted by the members of the class on those who were usually corrected for maladaptive behavior. The students in the class began to make attempts to regulate not only their own behavior, but also the behavior of other members of the class. Packard (1970) studied members of four elementary classes. In all the classes observed it was found that the introduction of a group contingency depending upon the proper attention and behavior of all, raised the level of attention and reduced the level of misbehavior. When the entire class would suffer for the misbehavior of one or two students there was great pressure placed on each member. No student wanted to be the one who prevented the others from receiving a reward.

In summary, these studies showed that peer pressure plays an important role in correcting maladaptive behavior. If rewards for the entire class depend upon good or appropriate behavior of the entire class, then all members will be on the lookout for those individuals who ruin it for everyone else. The class will take appropriate actions against these students. These may be verbal reprimands and criticism, or threatening gestures and glances. On the other hand, peer reinforcement may include praise, admiration, imitation and attention. The best method of using peer reinforcement is to instill in the minds of all the members of the class the idea that one student can deprive the entire class of a reward. When the student understands that his behavior, as part of a team, will either enhance or decrease the chances of rewards, then the maladaptive behavior will often be corrected. Peer reinforcement can work towards the basic need of everyone, the need to be accepted and the need of approval. Using this need for acceptance, and the fear of rejection, peer reinforcement may be used very effectively to correct maladaptive behavior.

Group Contingencies

Many studies have shown that reinforcements given to the class rather than the individual student could be successful in generating peer pressure on the behavior of deviant classroom members. Several of these studies were reported earlier in this chapter, under the subheadings "studies on social incentives" and "peer reinforcement and pressure." Coleman (1969) outlined a plan for an interscholastic academic olympics that could be structured on a group contingency basis. This idea has been implemented in various sections of the country. Sectional school-team champions are given an expense-paid trip to South Florida where the scholastic olympic games are held. Subjective reports by the initiators of the plan report it to be highly motivating and very successful, with a new breed of big man on campus emerging in the participating high schools.

Grieger (1970) reports an example of group contingency that occurred as part of the regular consultative services to Greendale Tutorial Day School, in Devon, Pennsylvania. Their teacher complained to the consultant about her students' rudeness. She was particularly concerned that most children "picked on" one child, Randy, primarily by directing their rude behavior toward bim. After eliciting the cooperation of the teacher, aides kept records of one week to determine the frequency of the undesirable behaviors. Calling-out averaged forty per ten-minute period (1440 per day and 7200 for the entire baseline week).

A reinforcement program was then devised. A child was automatically given an M&M candy at the end of each ten-minute period provided he did not hit or punch another child, make a disruptive noise, or call another child a name. As social consequences, the teacher ignored any inappropriate behaviors and immediately attended to a child when he raised his hand. If no child lost his reward during a period, each student was given two M&M's. The reinforcement period ran for two weeks. Results showed that the frequency of each inappropriate behavior decreased substantially in the first week of reinforcement. By the fourth week there were 82, 94, 91 and 99 percent reductions in hitting, spraying, name calling, and calling-out, respectively, from the base-rate week.

While this was not a formal study with a return to baseline and then a reinstatement of gain, results showed the efficacy of utilizing behavior modification principles in bringing about specific change in the behaviors of an entire class. Now, certainly, one would wonder how effective distributing M&M's would be with a class of regular high school students. Well, that particular consequence of group contingency would probably have little or no positive effect on students this age; but certainly teacher non-attention to certain inappropriate behaviors could have an effect on the entire group. Instead of candy, perhaps a free reading period, project time, or rap-session time could be made a consequence of appropriate group behavior.

One other study involving the manipulation of peer influence was conducted by Evans and Oswalt (1968) and involved twenty-two students from a fourth-grade spelling class. Two experimental subjects (S1 and S2) were selected by the classroom teacher and the other twenty students served as control subjects. The teacher announced daily, five minutes prior to the morning recess, that the class would be dismissed for recess immediately if S1 could correctly spell a specified word or words. If his spelling of the word was incorrect, classwork was continued until the customary dismissal time. During latter weeks, the procedure was identical, with the exception that early dismissal was made contingent on S2's responses rather than S1's. The results clearly showed that the test performance of both S1 and S2 improved considerably when the experimental condition was discontinued; however, S1's performance eventually declined to its previous level relative to the control subjects.

In view of the preceding experimental data, it would seem reasonable to assume that acquisition of control over an individual's behavior by making a class-reinforcer contingent on the behavior of the individual is a treatment technique that lends itself to a variety of behavior and learning problems in the classroom. In addition to its versatility, the technique has the advantage of requiring very little of the teacher's time or energy. Tests and records would be necessary only to evaluate the effectiveness of the procedures. Hopefully, these features will serve to make the technique both effective and practical in the regular classroom situation.

Schwieder's action research reported below illustrates the use of group contingencies to modify disruptive class behavior. Her students "punished the 'caller-outer' with scolding glances and sighs of disappointment." This study should be read for its implicit as well as explicit statements on classroom control with young children. As the author points out, her project could not determine the importance of group contingencies by themselves, because of a host of other positive interacting factors.

Decreasing the Calling-out Behavior of a Second-year Regular Class

by

Marion S. Schwieder

Purpose. The purpose of this research project was to decrease the calling-out behavior of the subjects when (1) the teacher was speaking, (2) when a question had been asked by the teacher, and it was indicated that the children should raise their hands, (3) when a child was speaking, and (4) when the children had been asked to work quietly. The purpose of the project was also to substitute calling out behavior with hand-raising behavior.

Subjects. The twenty-eight subjects (fifteen boys and thirteen girls; twenty-three white, three Puerto Rican, and two black) were members of a second-grade, self-contained classroom. Before the project was started, two of the subjects were mild discipline problems. All others were easy to work with and seemed to enjoy school tasks.

Procedure. The teacher-experimenter (E) spent thirty minutes each day (10:45 to 11:15) for five days gathering the baseline data. The data was collected while E was teaching reading to the entire class. Everytime a child called out without raising his hand and waiting to be recognized, a mark was recorded on a small tablet carried by E.

On the sixth day the program was begun. Before the first lesson of the day, the children were told that E was going to give them a big party (ice-cream, cake, pretzels, play games, etc.) if they did not call out more than five times during the day (a class total of five). From previous experience with the children E knew that a party could be a motivating factor.

Specific rules were given for when the children *could* call out, and when they *could not* call out. To help the children distinguish when they could and could not call out in response to a teacher question, the E raised her hand when she wanted the children to raise theirs. The specific behavior rules were thereafter gone over everyday of the program, although not always at the beginning of the day.

The children were given ample time during the day to express their thoughts and experiences, so that there was really no need to call out. They had one-half hour of "free time" as soon as they entered school in the morning, they were allowed to talk while passing out papers, they could whisper to their neighbors when both had completed assignments, and they had several two-minute "talk times" during the course of the day. Also, every effort was made to call on the child who had raised his hand, or to let him know that he would soon be called on.

The party was not the only reinforcement available. Praise had been a social reinforcement to the children before the project was begun. It had often been used to speed children in getting ready to work, in completing papers neatly, and so forth. Praise such as "Very good! I like the way you raise your hands," "You're so polite today," was used to reinforce children who raised their hands. At times they were praised as members of a group, and at times, individual children were praised.

If a child did call out, no direct comment was made by E, but a mark (which did not indicate *who* called out) was recorded on the tablet carried by the teacher. Gradually, the recording of the mark became a punishment to the children. They all were able to observe the act of recording the mark, and after they realized the marks were "strikes" against them, they punished the "caller-outer" with scolding glances and signs of disappointment. The children were never shown the marks they were accumulating throughout the day, as E felt the promise of a party would no longer be effective if they knew they had already accumulated five or more. However, starting the second week of the reinforcement program, E (at the beginning of the day) told the children how many marks they had received the day before and discussed the benefits of a party, and the possibility of only getting five marks that day.

Social Reinforcement

Token Ec.

Discussion of Results. The number of times the children called out gradually decreased. E felt that the decrease was a result of (1) specificity about when and where not to call out, (2) frequent praise by the teacher, (3) punishment from the class if one did call out, and (4) the promise of a party if only five call-outs were accumulated. The part played by each factor can not be exactly determined from the project.

The goal of five call-outs per day was not reached. Consequently, E decided to modify the program and continue it until the goal was reached, or until E was very satisfied with class behavior. By the third week of the reinforcement program, it became apparent that three students were doing most of the calling out, so E decided to start individual behavior modification programs with the three persistent "caller-outers." For a brief time, each of these students received a piece of candy and praise everytime he raised his hand to speak. Any call-outs made were recorded by name on the tablet and counted as part of the class total. When it became possible, they were put on an intermittent reward schedule, until social reinforcement was all that was necessary to maintain hand-raising behavior. Since candy was given to the three special children, candy was also used as a reward for the rest of the class, instead of a party. Candy was very desirable to the children, and since it was more immediate than a promise of a party, it was probably more motivating. When the calling-out behavior decreased, candy was given out on an intermittent schedule, along with frequent praise and the daily review of specific rules. The intermittent reward schedule was continued until E felt the calling-out behavior was sufficiently weakened, and the hand-raising behavior was strong enough. The decision was made on the basis of the data collected (recorded call-outs) and E's satisfaction with class behavior. Social reinforcement became the only reinforcement necessary to maintain desirable behavior.

Specific Techniques for Classroom Application

The potential interventions based on the material in this chapter include a variety of techniques in which the teacher works with the student in a direct, personal way. As used in the present framework, an intervention stemming from social reinforcement or group contingencies refers to an event in which all of the participants gain meaning from their active participation in the relationship (Catterall, 1970).

The regular classroom teacher may attempt to help students either increase or decrease their sensitivity to specific stimuli by employing one of the following procedures. If the child is a perfectionist, and consequently becomes easily frustrated, the teacher could introduce small doses of disappointment to the student to develop his tolerance. If a student exhibits great anxiety toward an object or situation, the teacher can attempt to reduce the anxiety by using relaxation techniques along with successive approximations. If the student's problem is one of coping with interpersonal relationships, e.g. meeting and conversing with strangers, the teacher can help him to develop social skills which will aid him through specific situations. Teachers can also help students to increase their sensitivity to problem situations by having them act out and then discuss various roles.

The teacher can assist in changing behaviors through intervention based upon group interactions or discussions. Role playing or rehearsal can again be employed, using the group to aid the individual in gaining insight into his problem. Games which involve the child in a group, can help the individual to learn to use specific rules to make decisions and to see the consequences of his decisions as well as helping the group gain proficiency in decision-making.

Social Reinforcers as a Beginning and End

When it becomes obvious that some type of practical intervention is necessary to reduce disruptive behavior, a choice must be made as to what method of reinforcement can best be used; there are many types of reinforcements. Perhaps the highest goal in behavior control is self-control, when an organism can maintain his own behavior. Until that stage is reached, the complexity and power of the modification program will be proportionate to the type of reinforcer employed. Thoreau's suggestion to "Simplify, simplify, simplify" is still a good rule. Start with the easiest type of reinforcer to administer, then work your way up. Material reinforcers (food, toys) and secondary reinforcers (money, tokens) have all been used in various situations along with social reinforcement.

In terms of practicality, social reinforcers prove to be the least expensive and least troublesome incentive. If behavior can be effectively manipulated by use of social reinforcement alone, no other type of incentive is necessary. When material or secondary reinforcers are employed, coupling them with social reinforcement is recommended to increase their success and to prepare students to be solely reliant upon praise, and eventually, self-management.

The preceding studies demonstrate the effectiveness of social incentives in the classroom. The practicality of social incentives is an important advantage. The studies cited give strength to the assertion that teachers can be taught systematic procedures and can use them to gain more effective behavior from the pupil. This means that the use of social incentives should become an integral part of a teacher's classroom behavior.

Not only does this make the teacher a more effective guide for children but it gives the teacher more time to devote himself to classroom activities and subject matter.

How does this give the teacher more time when he has to be circulating constantly throughout the room praising good behavior? The teacher does not have to praise the pupils constantly once the initial introduction of social incentives is past and the program is established. At this point, intermittant reinforcement takes over. This means that the child is weaned from receiving constant praise to experiencing teacher approval only a few times a day. This can be effective because at this point in the program, a supportive atmosphere has been established in the classroom, and the teacher is seen as warm and helpful.

What all this means to the elementary classroom is that verbal praise or reinforcement is an effective incentive, one that is more effective in some situations than in others. A major problem with formulating theories in regard to positive verbal reinforcement is that under certain conditions it can increase disruptive behavior. One common example of this situation is the student who is ridiculed by his peers for receiving positive teacher attention. An obvious way to avoid this problem and also enhance the reinforcement is to praise the student quietly and privately. Nevertheless, there is a great need for further and more controlled research in the area of positive social reinforcement in order that teachers, in modifying classroom behavior, learn when, how and with whom to use it most effectively.

Many teachers use praise because it is practical, usable, and brief; it does not take up space in the classroom as do a token economy and back-up reinforcers. Also, there is no question of negative psychological effects as with blame. The best advice this author can offer teachers is that in modifying classroom behavior, try positive verbal reinforcement first; see if that by itself offers satisfactory results. Only when this procedure proves ineffective should more powerful, but costly and time-consuming methods such as a token economy be attempted.

References

Andrews, H. "The effects of group contingencies and reinforcement on classroom behavior." *Dissertation Abstracts International,* July (1971), *32,* 227–28.

Barrish, H., M. Saunders and M. Wolf. "Good behavior game: Effects of individual contingencies for group consequences on disruptive behavior in a classroom." *Journal of Applied Behavior Analysis* (1969), *2,* 119–24.

Catterall, C. D. "Taxonomy of Prescriptive Interventions." *Journal of School Psychology* (1970), 8 (1), 5–12.

Clark, C. A. and H. J. Walberg. "The use of secondary reinforcements in teaching inner-city school children." *Journal of Special Education* (1969), *3,* 177–85.

Coleman, J. S. Incentives in American education. Paper presented at Brookings Seminar on Incentives in Public Policies, John Hopkins University, February 1969.

Dickinson, D. "Changing behavior with behavioral techniques." *Journal of School Psychology* (1968), *6,* 278–83.

Evans, G. and G. Oswalt. "Acceleration of academic progress through the manipulation of peer influence." *Behavior Research and Therapy* (1968), *6,* 189–95.

Grieger, R. "Behavior modification with a total class: A case report." *Journal of School Psychology* (1970), *8,* 103–6.

Madsen, C., W. C. Becker and D. Thomas. "Rules, praise and ignoring: Elements of elementary classroom control." *Journal of Applied Behavior Analysis* (1968), *1,* 139–50.

O'Leary, K. D. and W. C. Becker. "The effects of the intensity of a teacher's reprimands on children's behavior." *Journal of School Psychology* (1968–1969), *7,* 8–11.

Packard, R. G. "The control of classroom attention: A group contingency for complex behavior." *Journal of Applied Behavior Analysis* 1970, *3,* 13–28.

Schmidt, G. and R. Ulrich. "Effects of group contingent events upon classroom noise." *Journal of Applied Behavior Analysis* (1969), *3,* 171–79.

Thomas, D. R., W. C. Becker and M. Armstrong. *Operant Conditioning in the Classroom.* New York: 1971, 166–83.

7

Contingency Contracting: From Teacher to Self-control

Several chapters in this book have shown that a student's behavior is affected by consequences administered by his teacher or classmates. The next step is to inquire if the child can be taught to choose his own curriculum and reinforcements in order to facilitate academic and social gains. The questions about self-management are extremely important if the teacher is interested in producing long term behavior change, even after the withdrawal of social or tangible reinforcers.

In some contingency programs a formal or informal contract is drawn up between the teacher and the student or class. While most studies and examples in this chapter will describe contracts with an individual student, it should be readily apparent that the procedure could be extended to the entire class without undue problems arising. The contract may be a short statement by the teacher stating the consequences to be gained by certain behaviors, or it may be written out and agreed upon by both teacher and student. Or students may have major responsibility for all steps in the contracting procedure. The contract system is geared for self-determination. The student and the teacher sit down and work out what the student should work on, how long it should take him to do it, and the date of completion. A homemade contract is used and is signed by both the teacher and the student. This has proven to be a worthy innovation. The students enjoy the fact that they have something to say about their learning activities and how long they will spend doing it. It teaches them responsibility for their work, as well as something about contracts that will affect their future lives. It also makes them more aware of their abilities, since they must make judgments about themselves with this system.

The different types of contingency contracts are based upon the consistent application of two principles: (1) a desirable behavior is more likely to gain in strength if it is followed by a reward each time it occurs, and (2) students can learn more effectively if they are allowed greater freedom and involvement in the decision-making process of the learning situation.

Basic Rules of Contingency Contracting

Homme (1969) has set out ten basic rules for contracts. Both teachers and students are no doubt familiar with Grandma's Law which states, "First eat your potatoes and vegetables, then you can have your dessert." Homme's rules succinctly describe what the necessary preconditions are for Grandma's Law to be effective.

1. The contract payoff (reward) should be immediate.
2. The initial contracts should call for and reward small approximations.
3. Reward frequently with small amounts.
4. The contract should call for and reward accomplishment rather than obedience.
5. Reward the performance after it occurs.
6. The contract must be fair.
7. The terms of the contract must be clear.
8. The contract must be honest.
9. The contract must be positive.
10. Contracting as a method must be used systematically (p. 18—21).

For a more complete explanation of these rules and the general procedures of contracting, see Homme's *How to Use Contingency Contracting in the Classroom.*

There is only one regulation in the classroom—learning must be taking place and nothing should be done by anyone that would interfere with anyone else's learning. Classroom management problems can be handled in a mature and democratic fashion. If a student seriously misbehaves or has a problem with another student, a courtroom situation can be quickly set up with a jury, a judge, and a prosecuting and defense attorney. After the evidence is presented and the jury makes a decision, the judge (teacher) passes sentences. The jury can recommend mercy. This approach to discipline has been proven very successful. The students accept responsibility for their negative behavior much more readily and consider it to be "fair play." It also teaches something about our judicial system, and respect for the judicial process.

From Teacher, to Mutual, to Student-Control

All competent teachers would like their students not only to learn subject matter, but also to develop strong character. Such attributes as self-discipline and initiative would be indicative of this character development. Student contracting, or self-contracting, offers a promising beginning to teaching and developing these attributes. Unfortunately, few studies have been made in determining the difficulties to be expected in assisting the student toward the eventual goal of self-control. The following is an analysis of the way teacher contracting may be shaped to self-contracting (Homme).

In teacher-controlled contracts the amount of the task required and the reinforcement offered are determined by the teacher, while the major function of the student is to accept the conditions. In the self-contract the student sets all conditions of the contract, including agreement to his own contract. Obviously there are a number of transitional steps where both teacher and student are involved in determining the terms of mutual contracts. The terms involve setting up the task to be completed, and the consequent reward. Initially the teacher may share decisions on tasks but assume major responsibility for reinforcers, or vice versa. The second transitional step involves mutual control by the teacher and student of both task and reinforcement, or that each contractor maintain major responsibility for either task or reinforcement decisions, but not for both. The final transition is a reversal of the initial step, with the student now sharing one decision with the teacher, while assuming full control of the remaining decision, e.g., the student decides on the reinforcer but the teacher jointly controls the amount of task with the student.

In teacher-controlled contracts and in the first transitional stage, the major change from traditional classroom procedures is that the student, presented with the pre-packaged program, has the choice of which task he wishes to do at the time. Although the teacher retains much of his command of the learning situation, these initial stages of contingency contracting do require much greater self-discipline on the part of the student. Often the student can select his work location, his starting and stopping time for particular tasks, and part of the responsibility of the evaluation process his own performance requires.

The following action research by Scull illustrates mutual contracting by both teacher and student. The study was completed while the teacher was enrolled in a course on educating behaviorally disordered children. Regular classroom teachers should note the types of reinforcers Scull was able to effectively utilize.

Price Setting as an Incentive in Behavior Modification

by

Nick Scull

The purpose of this research was to attempt to introduce a measure of freedom into the value of the children's work in terms of a token reinforcement system. It was hoped that in allowing the children to bargain for the amount of chips they would earn, they would realize more satisfaction from it, and thereby increase their output.

The Group. The students were five children in a class of eight, comprising the upper elementary emotionally disturbed class. Three of the members were eliminated from the study for either having extended absences, or for not being present in the classroom for the entire day. The five in the study represented a wide range of behavior, from introverted to acting out, and spent a major portion of their days working on individualized materials.

The Method. The experiment was done in two parts of four weeks each. In the baseline period, the students were assigned work, and a price was set by the teacher. The teacher attempted to be fair in estimating the value, but the child had to accept it on a take it or leave it basis.

In the experimental period, the child would complete the task and then bring it to the aide or teacher, and bargain for his payment. There were two understandings that developed: The first was that the teacher would not accept the first offer if it was too high. The second was that as the amount of chips demanded increased, the prices of the reinforcements went up, and the reverse if the demands went down.

In both the baseline and experimental periods, a daily tally of each child's earnings was kept. The child with the most chips *earned* was the "messenger" or "monitor" for the following day. The child who had earned the most chips for the week received a prize on

Friday, when all chips reverted back to the "bank." In both cases the reinforcers were things such as pretzels, playing with the hamster, using the tape recorder, restroom, etc.

Tallies were kept of each individual's earnings, and the individual's average earnings were computed for both the baseline and experimental period. The means of these averages were determined, and the individual's performance was compared to the group's norm in terms of standard deviations from the mean of the group.

A side effect was how "inflation" affected the average of the group during the experimental period. "Inflation" was turned back by raising the prices of the reinforcers.

Results. With some minor deviation, *output*, in terms of chips earned, *improved slightly* for four of the five children. This improvement ranged from one-half to one standard deviation (S.D.). The fifth child dropped back approximately one S.D. The relationships in terms of chips earned stayed the same between these four, while the child who had previously been in fourth place dropped to fifth. The downward trend in the chips earned by the total group during the experimental period indicated that raising the prices curbed the inflation.

Discussion. The relatively simple statistical analysis seemed to support the thesis that freedom of choice increased individual's earnings. Admittedly, this is not the same thing as output in terms of actual work, but it makes the teacher feel more comfortable in assuming the children are getting what they would consider fair value for their work. The spread of scores was illustrated to be much larger during the experimental period, showing that the freedom had either strong positive or strong negative effects on some of the children. Even though the relationships stayed the same among the children, the standard deviation almost doubled between the two periods.

In summary, the experimental evidence indicates that freedom to bargain increases motivation in some children, and raising the prices of reinforcements will act as a natural means to control a token system.

When the contracting system evolves into the last transitional stage, and then into student-controlled contracts, the student takes charge of all decisions, including subject matter content; in other words, the student has major responsibility for designing the problem, asking the questions and evaluating his answers. In this stage of what might be called total freedom, a major adjustment for both student and teacher is their view of the relationship between time and efficient production. With both command and responsibility for the learning process, it will normally take longer for the student to organize learning activities which seem scattered or haphazard, into what the student deems to be orderly and reasonable for him. Once this plateau is reached, creativity may begin.

Self-Specification of Tasks

One response incentive is self-determined goals. Kennedy (1968) studied the math performance of third- and fourth-graders in a low socioeconomic area. Subgroups of children were instructed to follow four different procedures: (1) do their best, (2) set their own goals, (3) follow goals set by the teacher, and (4) the control group was given no goal-setting instructions. Students given self-set goals or specific goals by the teacher did better than the other two groups.

A long range goal of education is that learning will eventually lead to intrinsic rewards. Self-management of response is especially important because it leads to self-managed learning. The following research illustrates the use of self-management as a learning incentive. Campbell and Chapman (1967) found that students in a student-controlled study group showed increases in appreciation for both geography and for self-directed instruction; the appreciation was significantly greater than for the comparison group designated as program-controlled, and given a study plan for the course. The academic performance of both groups, however, was about equivalent after eight months.

Many of us have unknowingly practiced behavior modification upon ourselves when we have said that only after we have completed a rather odious task will we allow ourselves to engage in more desirable behavior. This is an example of the Premack principle which is as follows: If an organism is more likely to engage in behavior B than in behavior A, then behavior A can be made more probable by making the opportunity to engage in behavior B contingent upon the performance of behavior A. Another example of the Premack principle is demonstrated in the Lovitt and Curtiss study (1969). They found some evidence to suggest that when children themselves decided that they should complete certain academic tasks before allowing themselves to play in a free-activity area, the probability of their engaging in academic tasks increased.

Student Record-Keeping

Less complex methods of record-keeping will often be needed to implement a behavior modification program by teachers with large classrooms or by teachers who lack the experience or time for more complex recording. For more simplified recording methods for the teacher, Blackham and Silberman's *Modification of Child Behavior* (1971) is recommended.

It was suggested earlier that academic goals, rather than deviant social behavior as the target for a behavior modification program may have several advantages. Academic response rates are often times easier to record, to define, and to teach to teacher aides. In many cases even teacher aides will not be available, but several studies have shown that students can be employed successfully in this role. Students may serve as classroom monitors and record disruptive behavior (Minuchin, Chamberlain and Graubard, 1967) or they may serve as correctors or recorders of work assignments. The aides may be students from the same class or older students from another class. (Often students find this role highly reinforcing, and will work for this privilege).

Minuchin's study utilized an intervention curriculum designed to explore ways of enabling six delinquent children to overcome their deficits. The pupils alternately assumed a role of observer and were coached to rate the other children's ability to respond to the teacher. They enumerated behaviors which enhanced or interfered with learning. Small monetary rewards were given for points received in the classroom, and the judges were also rated and given points. After each judgment, observers made detailed oral reports to the class specifying their observations and reasons for giving or withholding points. Based on the authors' clinical observations, marked increases were noted in the children's ability to maintain attention and handle mechanics of dialogue and language.

Duncan (1968) taught teenagers to analyze their own selected behavior targets by recording and plotting daily rates of occurrence. They measured precisely the effects of altering their environments with contingent consequences; they found that the more precisely they measured, the more successfully they managed their behavior.

Improved effects from recording one's own behavior were reported by Broden, Hall and Mitts (1971). The authors suggest that self-recording may be particularly useful for teachers of large-size classrooms where they can seldom find time for dealing with each child's behavior. The Broden study found self-recording initially influential in increasing study time and decreasing talking out behavior; however, the effect diminished with one child presumably because no contingencies were ever applied to differential rates of talking out.

In summary, within each area of work, whether it be math, reading or whatever, the student can keep a record of his achievement and progress. This usually takes the form of a bar graph indicating the percentage of successful responses or reading rate depending upon the particular area of work. It is the student's responsibility to keep these charts up to date. This system gives the student an immediate graphic representation of his progress and achievement which, for some students, is a reward in itself.

This is also an attempt to motivate the student to compete with himself rather than his classmates.

Self-evaluation and Reinforcement

The Lovitt and Curtiss study tested the performance consequences of contracts in which reward contingencies were specified by the student in contrast to teacher-specified contracts. The authors reported better results when the student decided his contingencies than when the teacher specified them. However, the student did tend to reward himself at a higher rate than the teacher usually did.

Several experiments were conducted in which students rewarded themselves for achieving some performance standard. McMains (1969) gave verbal instructions to one group, establishing the score they should achieve before they rewarded themselves with tokens. A second group observed an adult play the game and reward himself. A third group received both conditions, while a control group was given neither. The combined verbalization-model group produced higher standards for self-reward than the other groups. Bandura and Kupers (1964) performed a similar experiment and achieved similar results. These studies suggest that if the teacher reinforces only those behaviors which meet certain high standards it is likely that the student will model the teacher's behavior and will later be self-approving of only those high standard behaviors. Both studies point out the important role of modeling in the development of self-reinforcing behavior. It should be emphasized that these self-management skills must be engineered or taught; they do not occur fortuitously.

As a further motivational technique, natural rewards can be used. A particular student may enjoy working on certain activities either academic or recreational. This is a perfect resource to motivate the individual student. A reward is very relative to the individual—what serves as a reward to one student may be meaningless to another. When the student completes a certain activity, he is allowed to take part in an activity that he particularly enjoys. The skillful teacher can use many things as motivational rewards that are a natural part of the classroom.

It should be clear from the studies on the effects of modeling on self-management that there is a difference between one's self-reinforcement and one's self-evaluation behavior. The two characteristics seem to be quite distinct in certain children, perhaps due to past learning experiences. By teaching self-management skills these traits may become more congruent with each other as well as help the student to work independently of his teacher.

Adjusting Nonfunctioning Contracts

If, after evaluating his ongoing data, the teacher determines that his contingency contract is not functioning as he anticipated, then he should re-examine the following components of the contracting system. Did the teacher adequately measure the skill level of the student upon entry into the program? Were materials corresponding to these goals made available? Finally, the teacher must ask himself if reinforcers appropriate to each student were made available as rewards for successful completion of tasks.

If the teacher can answer affirmatively to the above questions, very likely the problem arises due to a contract which is too short or too long. If the contract is too short and the student finishes his assignments before the expected time then the contract can be lengthened; the tasks can be made more difficult, or more tasks at the same level can be added. Either way, the student should be made to feel that this is a step forward, a promotion. If the student consistently fails to complete a contract which is too lengthy, then the number of tasks should be shortened or more simplified tasks substituted.

Conclusion

Student contracting is a procedure whereby each student determines the specific activity, the specific length of time, and the specific amount of material to be studied. Upon discussing this agreement with the teacher, and signing the contract, the student becomes obligated to live up to its terms. All of this is subject to the approval of the teacher, but he only intervenes when there is an obvious disparity in the selection. This is usually uncommon. The teacher actually just decides on the level of instruction to be received—a necessary condition.

A feeling of accomplishment and success can be experienced through the successful completion of contracts. The student succeeds in areas of his own choosing. This should give him confidence to attempt other areas. In this manner, it is hoped the student will gain a better self-image and better academic and social adjustment.

Variety is encouraged; the student selects the specific area in which to work, depending on his current mood, motivation and interest. If, after completing his present contract, he would like a change of activity or a different program for the same specific skill area, he simply writes a new contract for the desired change. The individual student determines his own variety. He determines when he works on the activity, how long he works on it, and how much of it he wants to do. It is anticipated that the student's interests will expand and, then too, his educational achievements.

Self-determination is promoted by the fact that the activities in which the individual student engages are of his own choosing. It is hoped that the student will grow to understand his limitations and strengths. Since he will work only on material in which he can succeed, the student is encouraged to work in areas of difficulty. The assumption here is that if the student succeeds in previously frustrating areas, he will learn to appreciate their relevancy. Obviously this is a highly individualized program and can deal with a wide deviation of disabilities. In operating such an individualized program, instruction on the present achievement levels of each child must be provided, which allows him to progress at a comfortable rate, and provides a stimulating reinforcement system that will motivate him to do so.

While self-management objectives may not be the most effective motivators for a specific child at a particular developmental level, the teaching of self-management skill is an extremely important educational goal. Many children are likely to react favorably to the increased opportunity to determine their own educational destiny by increasing their own motivation for academic achievement.

References

Bandura, A. and C. J. Kupers. "Transmission of patterns of self-reinforcement through modeling." *Journal of Abnormal and Social Psychology,* (1964), *69,* 1–9.

Blackham, G. J. and A. Silberman. *Modification of Child Behavior.* Belmont, California: Wadsworth publishing Co., 1971.

Broden, M., R. V. Hall and B. Mitts. "The effect of self-recording on the classroom behavior of two eighth-grade students." *Journal of Applied Behavior Analysis.* (1971), *4,* 191–99.

Campbell, N. and A. Chapman. "Learner control vs. program control of instruction." *Psychology in the Schools,* (1967), *4,* 121–30.

Duncan, A. D. "Self-application of behavior modification techniques by teenagers." Research Training Paper No. 11. Kansas City: Bureau of Child Research Laboratory, University of Kansas Medical Center, 1968.

Homme, L. *How to use contingency contracting in the classroom.* Champaign, Illinois: Research Press, 1969.

Kennedy, B. J. Motivational effects of individual conferences and goal setting on performance and attitudes in arithmetic. July, 1968.

Lovitt, T. C. and K. A. Curtiss. "Academic response rate as a function of teacher and self-imposed contingencies." *Journal of Applied Behavior Analysis* (1969), *2*, 49–53.

McMains, M. J., et al. "Children's adoption of self-rewarding patterns: Verbalizations and modeling." *Perceptual and Motor Skills* (1969), *28*, 515–18.

Minuchin, S., P. Chamberlain and P. Graubard. "A project to teach learning skills to disturbed, delinquent children." *American Journal of Orthopsychiatry* (1967), *37*, 558–67.

8

Peer Tutoring

One of the major points expressed in this book is that the key to learning for many children is individualized instruction. Yet we are faced with the dilemma that as class size increases, likelihood of having teacher aids or other paraprofessionals to assist the teacher often decreases. Of course one way of achieving this individualization is through computer-aided forms of programmed instruction and other types of technical hardware, but usually school systems have insufficient funds for these "frills." Before despairing, there is one sure way of surmounting the manpower problem posed by attempting individualization, and that is to have each pupil play the tutor role, in which he learns through teaching, and also be a tutee, in which he is being taught.

At this point problems of labels crop up—labels caused by the abundance of research and literature in this field and, at the same time, the abundance of phrases such as "pupil-pupil, teaching-learning teams" (Christine, 1971), "student-monitors" (Neisworth, 1969), "pupil-pupil learning" (Allen, 1970), peer-teachers and peer-managers, to name some.

While there are slight definitional differences in each, all terms imply the same concept—that of using peers as functional aids in the classroom, both special and regular, thus abetting the learning process for all involved. Not to be outdone, we shall use the labels "pupil-teacher" or "peer-tutor."

In contrast to the more machine-oriented approaches which are by necessity highly ordered and structured, the pupil-teacher model has the option of being much more informal, definitely more geared to the learning style of the individual child as well as the individual idiosyncrasies of the tutor. The pupil-teacher model also capitalizes on classroom heterogeneity, thus reversing a quandary into a solution for the teacher. In heterogeneous classes the wide range of academic abilities enables the teacher to obtain tutors from the same class. In homogeneous classes it may be necessary to acquire tutors from upper grades.

The number of students who require tutoring will vary for each class. In some cases it will be possible to divide the class into pairs, pair consisting of one child learning and another "teaching." In other situations the number of children in need of tutoring will be less than half, in which case two or more tutors can take turns working with the tutee as a pupil-teacher. This circumstance permits the use of volunteers for tutoring, an effective procedure. Occasionally, more than half the class will need tutoring. Then it is suggested that an upper grade class be established as tutors. If this is not possible, a very workable and exciting alternative is to have each tutor work with two or more children.

Roles of the Teacher, Tutor and Tutee

In the tutorial program, a classroom teacher finds himself in a strange and somewhat alien role. He is being asked to supervise a program in which he is to act more like an administrator than a traditional teacher. His opinions, though of value, should not set guidelines. He is being asked to draw on whatever teaching knowledge he possesses to see to it that others might possibly employ some of his teaching expertise as though it was their own. In essence, a teacher might come to view the one-to-one tutorial program as a usurpation of his authority. Because of this it is very essential, crucial in fact, that teachers who oversee tutorial programs consider themselves as administrators and do not try to impose their methods on those of either the tutee or the tutor.

If the teacher approaches the tutorial program with the wrong attitude, the program can end up a failure. However, there are benefits that perhaps outweigh the damage that can be inflicted on an insecure teacher. A teacher's role may expand from one of sole dispenser of knowledge to include that of resource person, manager of learning, or orchestrator of various teaching-learning activities. A teacher, by observing the relationship of the tutor to the tutee, may pick up helpful guides that he can emulate when teaching children. If a teacher is truly interested in children learning, there will be a certain sense of vicarious accomplishment that he will share with tutors and tutees alike. Quite often the tutor may get even more out of the one-to-one tutorial program than the tutee. This isn't really as hard to understand as it may seem if taken at face value. The tutor's position of importance may even override the teacher's, or whoever is overseeing the tutorial program; he is the liaison between the teacher and the tutee. His role is perhaps the most complicated of all persons involved. He must be overseer, teacher, friend, and confidant to the tutee. Being a peer, he can understand just what the values of his tutee are, better than many teachers. He must engender faith and trust in his charge, but at the same time be able to impart knowledge and command respect without trying to dominate. If the relationship between the tutor and the tutee is not harmonious, the tutorial program will undoubtedly fail.

The tutor's relationship with the teacher is important. It is hard for a tutor after acting as a teacher to subjugate his position of authority to another teacher. If the teacher is fulfilling his role, there is no need for the tutor to become intimidated by the teacher. As overseer, a teacher must at all times not only respect a tutor, but convey this respect without demeaning the tutor's role. Because he is acting as a surrogate teacher, the tutor might often feel just as important as the teacher (and he might well be). Because the tutor is still young, and his personality and emotional development not complete, a teacher can do almost irreparable harm if he in any way makes the tutor feel that he is not doing his job or not doing as good a job as he, the teacher, would do if the tutee were his charge.

As the go-between the teacher and the tutee, the tutor finds himself in the unenviable position of having to cater to the whims of two people. If the teacher is a skillful one, the tutor will consider his position one of overseer and instructor to his charge. If there is not a good relationship between the teacher and the tutor, the tutor could end up conveying directly any hostilities he feels toward the teacher to the tutee, thus defeating the program's entire purpose.

So far, I've concerned myself with the tutors and the teachers in the one-to-one tutorial program. In most of the tutorial programs the tutee is low man on the tutorial pole, therefore it is necessary to be somewhat cautious in dealing with him. Just as the teacher must not make the tutor feel his position is not important, the tutor must in turn accord the tutee the same respect he gets from the teacher. Also, the teacher must not make the tutee feel that because he is being tutored by one of his peers, he is not worthy of the same consideration the teacher accords the tutor. Damage can easily be inflicted to a tutee's ego and would be more severe than that done to a tutor's.

Every tutee will develop at his own rate, and learn at the pace that feels most comfortable to him. The teacher need not worry that the tutor will go too fast for the tutee. If this should happen, in all likelihood the tutee will feel no qualms about telling his tutor to slow down, or stop altogether until a point that has evaded him is made clear.

As overseer, the teacher should be sagacious enough to spot any instances of a tutor trying to either make a tutee feel inferior, or not up to par with his peer group. If a case like this should arise, the teacher finds himself in the position of keeping the tutor in check without damaging his self esteem or lowering his position in the eyes of his tutee. Without the teacher intervening, crises between tutor and tutee will often resolve themselves. Most tutees realize that the tutorial program is structured for their benefit, and seldom will they purposefully abuse the position of the teacher or their tutor.

As noted earlier in the paper, often the tutor derives more academically from the tutorial program than the tutee does. Nevertheless, the sense of accomplishment that the tutee feels as he learns can prove as worthwhile as the academic benefits achieved by the tutor. Even though the program is structured primarily for the tutee to learn, it can aid in his emotional development and maturation. If at first it appears the tutee isn't learning as rapidly as the teacher thinks he should, this is no cause for alarm. In many instances academic achievement isn't as essential to the learning process as the development of a well-integrated personality.

If emotional development and maturation seem to take precedence in the tutorial program, they can act as the basis for later learning and assimilation of materials presented to the tutee. Since in many of the programs the tutees are underachievers, they very well might have some emotional or psychological problem. If the program aids in helping correct these somewhat, it has done perhaps even more than it set out to do. A confused, despondent child cannot learn as rapidly as a well-adjusted one; therefore, if the child doesn't appear to advance rapidly academically, he may be emotionally retarded, and correcting that part of his development.

Recent History of Peer Teaching

Research in peer tutoring has been underway throughout the nation and the world for several years now. Actually, the technique has been in existence as long as teaching has been in practice, but it is only in the past decade or so that formal research studies have shown its value. For many years, the children in several Soviet schools have adopted students in other classrooms with whom to work. Britain has infant schools and junior schools where multi-age "family grouping" occurs. In Cuba, the Each One Teach One approach is applied.

In most programs and in the early tutoring programs in the United States, general emphasis has gone toward improving the learning of the recipient. Generally, findings indicated that though the recipient improved in his learning, no major breakthroughs were evident. But in the early 1960s, attention was directed to the potentially significant benefits that may be derived by the tutor. One-to-one tutorial programs, where instituted, have proved beneficial to tutors, tutees, and teachers. Tutees show improvement in national test scores. Teachers learn to be more administrative without impeding or retarding the desire of their pupils to learn. Tutors perhaps even more than the tutees or the teachers, end up getting the most out of the program; often their scores on national tests jump by as much as five grades.

Taking all this into account, it is not hard to understand why different sections of the country have begun to experiment with and use tutorial programs. Each program will have about it certain identifying characteristics. These characteristics will be peculiar to various regions, and dependent on the structures of the tutorial programs. These differences in tutorial programs become understandable and even helpful when one realizes that it is the differences inherent in children's learning capabilities that initiated one-to-one tutorial programs.

Many of the studies involved "normal" children in regular classes. Some, however, concentrated upon exceptional children, such as the program where behavior-problem children were used as tutors (the Maimonides learning rehabilitation program), and the program for withdrawn children (Glavin and Shoup, 1970) which utilized one peer-tutor for every three tutees. This study involved children in a special class who were withdrawing from regular classroom work. They seldom paid attention during group lessons, and rarely completed their work. Using two members of the class as pupil-teachers, the entire class engaged in a program designed to improve reading. For those being taught, there was an increase in reading speed, ranging from 5 percent to 60 percent greater than anticipated, compared with children in general. Both pupil-teachers made the greatest reading gains (1.4 and 2.6 years) as measured on the California Achievement Test, with a five month interval between pre- and post-tests.

Application of Peer-tutoring in a Behavioral Setting

As mentioned earlier, the peer-tutoring model can be either very informal and idiosyncratic or it can be highly structured and preplanned. The former approach can be quite successful in stimulating creativity and involvement in the program with junior high and senior high school students, but the more highly sequenced and ordered method is recommended for use with younger children. The following example of the procedures used in the Glavin and Shoup study will give the reader some notion of the amount of detailed planning necessary when combining the pupil-teacher model with a token reinforcement system. The procedure used involved a sequential presentation of individualized, brief, silent reading assignments as part of the total reading program. Each child was given immediate feedback through the assistance of a pupil-teacher. Motivational variables, in the form of a token reinforcement system, were systematically alloted for both successful readers and their pupil-teachers.

Selection of Pupil-teachers

The following considerations were made in selecting pupil-teachers. If a child was older, he would be used as a pupil-teacher with those children who were reading at a lower level. Another procedure was to make use of a pupil the same age as his peers, who was reading at least one level higher. In each case, the pupils were assigned to the pupil-teacher on the basis of personality, compatability, and reading level. Using two pupil-teachers, the teacher was freed to tutor any child who needed special assistance, or to act as a "rover," assisting children in their silent reading or vocabulary review.

Experience has shown that good academic students don't necessarily make better tutors. Emphasis in tutorial programs has shifted from academically excellent students to those who are trustworthy, dependable, and who show genuine concern for children.

If possible, the tutors sbould be older than the tutee, but this rule can be modified somewhat. In some cases when tutor and tutee are practically the same age, the benefits to both are greater than if one is older than the other. The one requisite when the tutee and the tutor are close to each other in age, is that the tutor be intellectually superior to his tutee.

The actual pairing of tutor and tutee depends on the individual goals of the program. In some programs there might be emphasis on the material to be taught; here it sometimes is beneficial to the tutees that the tutors be shifted frequently. Because there is going to be such a close social interaction between the tutee and the tutor, it is usually desirable that both come from the same neighborhoods and essentially the same backgrounds. In some programs, race and sex did not prove to be crucial factors; in others, they did. If the program hopes to attain a level of emotional and psychological development commensurate with the academic levels of achievement, then it is best that the same tutor and tutee almost always work together.

The Procedure Followed by the Pupil-teacher

A four-step chained sequence of responding was required: reading a vocabulary list, reading a two- or three-page portion of a story silently from the basal reader, reading orally a selected portion of the story to the pupil-teacher, and correctly answering a comprehension question selected by the teacher. If the pupil was able to complete this sequence successfully, a reinforcement was awarded. The child then continued to his next assignment in the text, repeating the procedure.

The first-step in the sequence involved a review of vocabulary words missed in the previous oral reading session. These words were checked by the pupil-teacher. After successful completion of this step the pupil returned to his desk for silent reading of the assigned selection. The goal for each child was to be challenged and moved along as quickly as possible with a minimum of frustration or discouragement. It was considered better for the teacher to make an assignment too short rather than too long. This enhanced the frequency of reinforcement which was an important consideration in the study.

The pupil proceeded to read orally eight lines of print in the assignment selected by the pupil-teacher. Missed words were written on a piece of paper by the pupil-teacher and became the new vocabulary words to be learned by the pupil. If the pupil missed more than two words in his oral reading, the pupil-teacher reviewed the words with him and asked him to return to his seat and study the same section again. If two or less errors were made, the pupil-teacher sent the pupil to the teacher for his comprehension question. The teacher had on file the comprehension questions covering the reading assignments in each child's text. If the child missed the question, he was assisted and encouraged by the teacher to reread the section silently. He then returned directly to the teacher for the comprehension question. Upon answering the question correctly, the pupil was reinforced with three poker chips and instructed to begin his next story.

One of the most important aspects of the tutorial program is time: time of day for the program, and allotted time for each session. Mid-morning has proved to be the best time for the program. At this time of day, children tend to still be alert and eager to learn. Those programs that were conducted during the latter part of the day seem to run into trouble because the children were more worried about going home than assimilating what was being taught. In most cases, a tutorial program should not be more than two hours long. Two hours of tutoring can be taxing for even a child with regular grades. For an underachiever, it can seem like an eternity.

Analysis of Reading Material

Basal readers at the appropriate level were divided into one, two and three page lessons according to the child's need for success and his ability with reading skills. The start of a lesson was signaled by a circle around the page number; the ending page was designated by an X on the page number. During the pupil-teacher procedure, which lasted seven weeks, the teacher was enabled to extend the silent reading lessons to thirty-five minutes per day, because the usual reading groups were not necessary.

Reinforcement System

In the pupil-teacher phase of the study the reinforcement factor was modified, making it solely contingent upon successful completion of the four-step sequence described earlier. Immediately after completing each assignment the pupil was given three tokens and instructed to begin his next sequence. The pupil paid his pupil-teacher with one of his three tokens. Since each pupil-teacher had three or four pupils he assisted, all children in the class could earn approximately an equal number of tokens, which usually varied from ten to eighteen tokens per reading period. At the end of the thirty-five minute silent reading period, the children exchanged their tokens for check cards. They could spend their check cards immediately or save them for a higher valued back-up reinforcer.

Teacher Evaluation

The teacher reported several advantages of this procedure. It allowed her to plan more efficiently for each day, while spending less time on this task. Therefore she was able to devote more time to other phases of the reading program. The results suggest that using same-age peers could be especially useful when a class is grouped on a heterogeneous basis, rather than on a chronological or achievement one.

Several problems were encountered. The pupil-teachers were not always found to be reliable in writing the mistaken oral reading words, and could not be depended upon as the sole source of vocabulary review words for the readers. There were several reasons for this. One of the pupil-teachers was a bright but immature seven-year-old who sometimes succumbed to fear of a pupil getting angry with him. The older pupil-teacher occasionally was swayed by his anticipated share of the reinforcement system. Several changes were adopted to counter the above problems during the second year of the program. Any new vocabulary in the next assignment was reviewed in the first step of the sequence. The teacher rotated more among the pupils, reviewing new and old vocabulary words, and assisting readers in their silent work. Finally, as more pupils improved, the number of children who could be used as pupil-teachers increased and the pupil-teachers for each day could vary.

The pupil-teacher technique appeared to incorporate several obvious advantages. It aided the pupils in mastery of material by providing an individualized system to check, control and reinforce their progress. It increased the pupils' motivation by allowing them to experience frequent success in continuous, purposeful activities. The children worked with a minimum of frustration and competed successfully with other members of the class because they worked at their own pace, receiving immediate reinforcement. Finally, the withdrawn children were spared much embarrassment because no response had to be given in front of the whole classroom, only in a one-to-one situation.

Implications

In discussing implications it would be best to determine who is affected by the use of peer-tutoring and just what the particular effects are. Thus far, the ramifications in terms of the teachers (that is the certified professionals and paraprofessionals) have not been touched on. In consultation with many teachers, both in primary and secondary schools and on the college level, the general consensus is that the use of peer-tutoring is an excellent solution to lack of manpower. Most teachers think highly about peer-tutoring, but are quite uneasy about seeing their *own* peers out of work.

Effects on the students are reportedly fairly positive. However, there are some elementary school students who say they would feel threatened by the fact that one or more students in their class or school could somehow assume a power over them that they believe should be reserved only for the teacher. Thus, two suggestions regarding teachers' and pupils' feelings might well be: (1) take necessary steps toward implementing the use of peer power in the classroom, but at the same time do not disregard very capable teachers who may be out of work at the present, and (2) arrange the program so as to control any unfair usurpation of power by students who would not handle that power in the most beneficial way.

Another effect of such a program might well be the reduction of peer-group tensions, which are sometimes produced unknowingly by classroom teachers who adhere to strict traditional roles in the classroom and do not allow any classroom participation by students other than responses to teacher-initiated questions and commands. Individualizing learning with the use of behavior modification, while at the same time letting students participate in both extremes of the teaching-learning process, could produce a simultaneous lowering of these peer-group tensions by effectively extinguishing their causes.

Still another effect would be simply the lessening of classroom costs. Besides alleviating the need for paid personnel, peer-tutoring also reduces many material costs. Christine (1971) maintains that "the program can be handled within one school with no additional operating costs" (p. 259). Coupled with the research indicating its success, lack of increased costs could be one of the most important factors in the peer-teaching program's favor.

Conclusion

Thus far, this chapter has attempted to review the basics and the ramifications of the problems educators face: It deals with the question: How can we facilitate learning in the best possible way, faced with the manpower and economic shortages that now exist in our school system? As in the attack of any problem, we must break up the question into component parts with which we can deal. Unfortunately, we are forced to set aside the economic problems and deal specifically with learning facilitation in terms of increasing manpower, while at the same time balancing, or possibly decreasing, monetary output.

Von Harrison (1971) seems to best sum up the views of most theorists and researchers when he says that instead of regarding tutoring as solely for primary students in academic trouble, we should think of it as a possible solution for many children, both in primary and secondary schools, which can benefit them whether they participate in the teacher's role or the learner's role.

It seems that implementation into a regular classroom is very possible, since much of the research has been done in terms of peer-teaching in the regular classroom. However, certain cautions must be observed. The peer-tutor model can fail. Without wise and careful preplanning and supervision by the teacher, it can become a program of reward for the bright child and humiliation for the slower students. Children can be forced to tutor instead of relying upon volunteers, or it can be a way for school systems to rely on peer-tutors rather than paid staff. Tutors can teach in a harmful way or teach things that are wrong. Teachers may either feel incapable of organizing and supervising a peer—tutoring program or they may feel threatened by successful peer-tutors. In short, the peer-tutoring model is by no means a simplistic technique. The underlying processes involved need to be identified and understood if the program is to successfully tap the potential of cognitive and emotional gain for both the peer-teacher and the child being taught.

Only after clearing away all the academic fluff have educators been able to recognize, or willing to admit, why the one-to-one, child-to-child tutorial program works. Probably the most significant aspect of the entire program is that children can learn more readily from another child because they don't view one another as authority figures. There can exist a closeness between children that an adult, especially a teacher, can't duplicate. This closeness may be more than a matter of age. It may also involve sex, race or socioeconomic background. Children can more easily empathize with children. At times, adults feel that they can teach children to read, but there is too much of the pedagogue in our relationship with children to be as effective as we could be.

When one child teaches another, there are so many variables at work that it is hard to single out any one factor as being superior to another in contributing to the learning process. Besides the closeness that one child feels toward another, there is simply the matter of one tutee modeling himself after the tutor. Children, it has been said, learn by imitation. This imitation process comes into play when a child is being taught to read by one of his peers. It is somewhat like the big brother syndrome children go through when growing up. Most of us, at some time or other, tried to model after some teenager we liked or admired; this also holds true in the one-to-one tutorial relationship.

The increase and great interest in peer-tutoring at this particular time should really not be greatly surprising. The concepts actually work along well with current trends. For instance, peer-tutoring does individualize the approach of teaching, provide teaching resources, make for a more cooperative learning situation, lessen competition, and enhance the participatory process. With increasing recognition today, educators are discovering that learning need not be a win-lose game in which some pupils presumably learn a great deal in competitive grading systems, and others do not. There is a definite need for these "classrooms without failure."

References

Allen, D. W. "Students as teachers." *Education Cassette Series, 116.* Chicago: Instructional Dynamics Inc., 1970.

Christine, R. O. "The pupil-pupil teaching and learning team." *Education* (1971), 9, 258–60.

Glavin, J. P. and M. L. Shoup, "The use of peers in teaching reading to withdrawn children." U. S. Office of Education Grant G3–06–062–063–1559 n.d.

Neisworth, J. T., S. L. Deno and J. R. Jenkins. *Student motivation and classroom management: A behavioristic approach.* Lemont, Pa.: Behavior Technics, Inc. 1969.

Staats, A. W. and W. A. Butterfield. "Treatment of nonreading in a culturally deprived juvenile delinquent: An application of reinforcement principles." *Child Development* (1965), 36, 925–42.

Von Harrison, G. "Structured tutoring." Brigham Young University, Department of Instructional Research and Development, 1971.

9

Self-Management in Learning

One of the goals of educational and socialization processes is the development of self-directed activity, i.e., independence. Of course, this does not exclude the desirability of mutual interdependence in the society, but such cooperation implies conscious control and mature choice on the part of participants, rather than helplessness and actual dependency.

A Controversial Aspect of Behavior Modification

One of the currently popular criticisms of behavior modification programs is concerned with the implications of outside agencies used in behavior control—the spectre of "Big Brother" and the subjugation of people's wills without their awareness, imposing on them greater dependency. Skinner (1971) has attempted to dismiss this argument by questioning the validity of words such as freedom, but it continues to be raised by proponents of free will and would-be controllers of their own destinies.

Self-management in Learning

Strictly speaking, one supposes all types of behavior modification would seek to free participants, if only from self-defeating behavior. But just as the infant moves toward increasing independence, and the wise parent appropriately relaxes control, so might contingencies be changed in the formal education process, toward increasing individual responsibility. In fact, that this should and does occur is affirmed by proponents of pass-fail and contract grading systems, independent study, and even of old fashioned "self-discipline."

Methods used include self-reinforcement, self-observation, response-manipulation and stimulus-control techniques. This chapter will consider their use primarily with the older student, for whom material reinforcement may not be feasible, and for whom verbal incentives may be of inconsistent value. For example, in a review of empirical studies, Kennedy and Wilcutt (1964) indicated the need for further clarification of the motivational effects of praise and blame on some students. One group of highly intelligent children showed no difference between the effects of praise and blame (Kennedy, et al., 1962), and others seemed not to be motivated even by praise. Kennedy and Wilcutt concluded that the reinforcement history of individuals is a variable which must be considered in assessing the influence of these incentives.

Using Judgment with the Behavior Modification Approach

The behavior modification approach is valuable only when used prudently, as a tool when it is needed, and only to the extent necessary. It aims at helping children develop behaviors for coping with life situations. The teacher should not lose sight of the goal of transferring behavior to the most natural situation possible. For example, a teacher should not use a material reward if a more "natural" reinforcement such as praise would be effective in the situation. The ultimate goal is to provide children with self-direction.

As stated previously, the behavior modification approach is criticized when its only emphasis is on the extrinsic aspect of the individual. Programs can sometimes ignore the vital part of learning based on the motivations of the student. Such situations in the final analysis deal only superficially with the student, instead of understanding the important underlying causes of his behavior. It is true that the classroom teacher has neither the time nor the training to analyze the "inner" self of each student, but it is possible for the teacher to secure a deeper understanding of the child.

The techniques of behavioral management, if seen in perspective with the much quoted "whole child" concept, can be valuable in the classroom. One way in which the teacher can manage behavior with respect to the intrinsic is to understand the concept and practicalities of response manipulation. Response manipulation is a type of behavioral control that focuses on inner motivations of action. It implies a group of incentives that rely on self-reinforcement instead of externally imposed contingencies.

Lipe and Jung (1961) state that response manipulation leads to the issue of self-managed learning. The possibilities of giving students self-direction is inherent in this concept. There are certain assumptions concerning the capacities and "rights" of students that supports the possibilities of giving students self-direction. R. E. Samples (1970) discusses these assumptions. He asserts that the student (at any level) has a background of experiences which far outweighs the curriculum for the year. For example, children beginning school have an average of five or six years experience behind them. Samples explains that by rewarding the student by drawing upon his experiences, you provide him with the chance to be an "authority." He is an authority concerning what he knows. This is a vital step in establishing a self-image.

Another assumption reflects the rights of the student. Samples states that the student is capable of making decisions about certain things that happen to him in his environment. Perhaps the capacity for self-direction assumes a certain emotional maturity and cognitive capacity; most students, however, even of lower intellectual and emotional capacities, can make certain decisions such as those based on their interests. In a completely extrinsically oriented environment, all decisions are made for the student. A democratic form of extrinsic coercion is realized when the student is given the option of choosing among the alternatives that the teacher provides. Samples states that this still does not completely reflect inner needs. The element of choosing between someone else's alternatives is often confused with true intrinsic decision-making. A condition based on true motivation would be one where the student must make choices between alternatives that he creates. This is the optimal condition that teachers should be aware of even though it may not seem practical for a sequentially developed curriculum.

Once the child trusts the environment, he will learn far more than in a situation in which he cannot relate. Samples states that in order to create an atmosphere of trust, the school must be involved in reaching more than only the cognitive aspect of the child. Education must be equally concerned with the affective aspect of the individual. This implies objectives that are not as easily evaluated. We cannot "test" this affective component but it must be considered and used by teachers in guiding classroom activities. Environments in which the students "coerce" themselves will allow this affective component to develop. Samples remarks that intellectualization and skill development are inevitable when children feel secure with themselves and their environment.

Characteristics of Self-direction

In looking at self-directed behavior we are also prompted to question what its components are so that these may be taught or learned, as the case might be. We are not likely to assume any longer that such components are simply innate. Winter and others (1968), on the basis of their studies with graduate students, believe they have identified some of these characteristics. They used an inductive approach to discover factors distinguishing high-change low-change students in their T-group courses. They found some interesting support for what might seem rather evident features; that those students able to make successful changes had well-developed awarenesses of the discrepancies between their real state of affairs and the ideal condition. Identity diffusion was a characteristic found to be incompatible with high-change behavior. This was inferred in Winter's study from statements of subjects indicating: (1) concern with reality, (2) feeling of playing a role, (3) vagueness about others' perceptions of the self, and (4) indecisiveness and lack of conviction.

One reason for unfavorable schedules of reinforcement sometimes found with self-monitored systems was a lack of norms and models for objective criteria. One way in which children internalize norms for self-standards of behavior is through observation of models. This implies social cues from peers or standards observed in adults. An observation of nursery school children by Masters (1969) indicated that these children took cues from one another for standards in reinforcing themselves. This study particularly observed conditions of unequal reinforcement. Some children were given fewer rewards than a peer, more rewards than a peer, or the same amount of rewards as a peer. Masters found that the child who received fewer rewards tended to indulge in high self-reinforcement. Following this trend, the children who received more rewards than a peer indulged in less self-reinforcement. Equal reward situations results in moderate conditions of self-reinforcement. Another finding of this study showed that girls showed higher self-responses than boys in both conditions of inequity such as more or less reinforcement.

Staats (1971) discusses the power of the model. This concerns not the power to administer external material rewards but the "power" that is measured by the attitudinal or emotional value of this person to the child.

The psychological implications involved in this concept are fairly complicated. Staats gives a simplified explanation of this idea but asks us to be aware of the larger scope of the concept. Stated simply, the child will be rewarded many times when he imitates people who have high reward value (in the emotional sense) to him. As a consequence his attitude toward these people will come to control his responses. The child will be "rewarded" by imitating these people who have emotional significance to him. Imitation behavior increases when the model has more "status" in the child's viewpoint. A person who is skilled would be a more effective model than an unskilled person. Also persons who can supply the child's emotional needs (affection, attention, understanding, praise, etc.) would be effective models.

The implications of these findings which deal with characteristics of persons capable of self-directed change, lead to several questions as to their relevancy to education. Do we help students define and express goals? Are we providing useful feedback of their program for them? How can we encourage the development of self-identity in students? Although an identity crisis occurs in adolescence, groundwork is laid in the formative stages. Can we facilitate the process by educational methods? Since older students are complaining of the lack of relevancy in their education, we can afford to experiment with alternatives. Volunteer work in community projects is an example of such an alternative. If we define and set the goals and reinforce the behavior we desire, are we really creating the conditions for the kind of maturation we say should occur? These questions are not new. But they are restated to examine their significance in the context of behavior modification theory.

Although dissonance probably will need to be maintained, it must not impose a sense of failure and hopelessness, thus making it aversive. This is the point Glasser made in his book, *Schools Without Failure* (1969). He recognized that teachers must also be permitted some self-direction and latitude in carrying out their ideas. They too are dominated by the atmosphere of grading and failure.

Self-direction might be desirable for graduate students and teachers, but can children be trusted to make wise choices? No one would advocate a complete turnover of training and education to children, but a certain amount of practice in self-management and control is vital for learning to be independent.

Self-imposed Contingencies

It has been mentioned that self-directing activities are more motivating than extrinsically imposed situations. An investigation of self-imposed versus teacher-imposed contingencies (Lovitt and Curtiss, 1969) has revealed that self-scheduling of events is associated with accelerated performance. This study was focused on one student who was attending a special class for behavioral disorders. The experiment involved three stages. The results revealed an increased academic response rate during stage two, the period of self-imposed contingencies. In stages one and three, involving teacher-imposed contingencies, the response rate was lower. The response rate increase was attributed to the contingency manager. These results would be more valid if the study involved more than one child. However, the implications of the positive value of the child being involved and making decisions is supported by other authors. Lovitt and Curtiss suggest that possibly certain factors such as a student plotting his own performance or being allowed to see a chart of his progress may be additional motivating factors. The idea of self-competition is inherent in this idea.

Samples (1970) mentions that the student is the best authority in what is motivating and relevant to him. Letting the students choose is an easy way for the teacher to receive cues on what is motivating to them. Samples mentions that it is even unfair to force the child to accept the curriculum without the element of choice. He states that this is most true in evaluation procedures which penalize the student for refusing to accept the curriculum's message. We need the element of standardization and stable objectives to be part of the curriculum, but, at the same time, we need workable methods of fitting curriculum to the child. The element of self-choice in the classroom is very valuable in this way.

High versus Low Probability of Behaviors

Premack formulated a concept involving a high versus low probability of behavior. This principle that has valuable application in the classroom states simply that high probability behaviors may serve as reinforcers for low probability behaviors. A high probability behavior is a behavior that an individual would be most likely to engage in if given the choice. Thus a low probability behavior would be the least likely choice. The Premack Principle has been tested and found valuable in different classroom settings. In one situation involving nursery school children, Homme and his co-workers (1963) had teachers use high probability behaviors as reinforcers. These were behaviors that were suppressed and punished previously before the use of this principle. The child received the opportunity to engage in a high probability behavior such as running around the room, pushing chairs, working on a jigsaw puzzle in exchange for engaging in a low probability behavior such as sitting and looking at the blackboard.

Teachers were surprised to find that such behaviors as kicking a wastepaper basket and throwing a cup across the room proved to be highly reinforcing activities once they were seen in the perspective of the Premack Principle.

With different groups of children at different ages and interests, the types of high probability responses vary. For example, in a study by Packard (1970) the desired responses of third, fifth and sixth graders included sitting next to a friend, using a private study booth, and being a teacher assistant. A positive aspect of using the Premack Principle is that it gives the teacher cues as to what activities the child enjoys. It can give the teacher greater insight into what motivates children for the purposes of directing teaching. It is also very practical as it includes situations that occur naturally in the classroom. Another aspect of this concept is that it gives the teacher more of a positive frame of reference in viewing all the behaviors of the child. Instead of viewing certain behaviors in a negative manner, these same behaviors can now be seen in a different light, as valuable reinforcers. Previously punished behaviors can become high probability behaviors or reinforcers. This is a more optimistic view than may have been held when a set of behaviors was labeled negative.

There are certain elements of self-monitored reinforcement systems that deserve particular cautions. In one study by Bandura and Perloff (1967), self-monitored and externally controlled reward systems were equally effective in sustaining favorable behavior when compared to conditions having no reward. One finding in this study was that children imposed unfavorable conditions of self-reward upon themselves. The standards that they set were often too high for the amount of work that they produced. There was an unfavorable work-to-reinforcement ratio which could lead to negative reactions concerning self-evaluation. High effort with little reward was found to result in negative self-regard evaluations. Bandura and Perloff mentioned a few cases when the child would maximize rewards with little effort costs to themselves. In these cases, frequent and easily obtainable rewards may become of less value than high effort rewards. This again leads to the issue of becoming satiated quickly with the rewards, resulting in the contingency system becoming ineffective.

Overevaluating capacities is sometimes a phenomenon of human nature. Almost always our aspirations begin higher than our capacities. It is admirable to set high goals and it is perhaps a positive factor for progress in the human condition. It is also very important to develop a realistic set of aspirations and to progress toward them within our capacity to perform. When students are allowed to set their own goals they often gain a better insight into their actual desires and capacities. In extrinsical-

Self-management in Learning

ly coercive environments the student learns to exert himself in the name of someone else's aspirations. As a result he may not have as much of a chance to understand his true capacities and goals. Self-evaluation of performance forces the student to look at himself.

Internal versus External Orientation

Self-direction is based on a cooperation of the person's "inner-self" interacting with his environment. Since behavior modification implies environmental control, we can question the implications of this control. What are the implications of an emphasis on either the external or internal orientation to the environment?

In one study, (Lefcourt, Lewis, and Silverman, 1968) the individual's control of the reinforcers was linked to the value the reward held for him. Externally controlled reinforcement gave the person the feeling that chance rather than his skill determined the outcome. A person in internally controlled conditions regarded skill as the important factor controlling the reinforcement. The idea of a person believing that his skill determines the outcome of his effort supports the practice of giving children opportunities for self-evaluation and self-reinforcement. Griffith and Kolb (1968) state that inherent in the idea of self-direction is the idea that the individual is given the responsibility to diagnose his problem, set a goal, and accomplish change through his own effort. An emphasis on the internal in this goal helps by causing the person to believe that he is the agent to effect change.

Research problems complicate the study of self-management. Not a great deal of research has been done, but this is being remedied, as interest in the area grows. The study of covert behaviors is especially difficult because these must be linked with changes in target behaviors. Long term effects are difficult to relate to a single variable. Self reporting is complicated by subjectivity, and therefore reliability is difficult to obtain. When experimenters set up research plans, their expectations may influence the subject. Subjects are understandably reluctant to reverse desired behavior once it has been acquired.

We want to insure that the process of education itself becomes the reinforcement of learning, or we want not to sever this relationship as it occurs naturally. Being alert for opportunities to encourage self-management may help cement this association. In reality, school situations are neither all externally controlled nor all internally controlled. If the final objective is self-control or self-direction, we should take heed of the area of response manipulation. It is worthwhile for the teacher to consider the values of self-set goals, self-management of rewards and self-determination of a study plan. As stated previously, school must prepare children for life. If the school environment relies too heavily on external control, it may create an artificial setting and fall short of giving children the tools to cope with reality.

References

Bandura, A. and B. Perloff. "Relative efficacy of self-monitored and externally imposed reinforcement systems." *Journal of Personality and Social Psychology* (1967), *7* (2), 111–16.

Glasser, W. *Schools without failure.* New York: Harper and Row, 1969.

Griffith, J. C. and D. A. Kolb. "Capacity for self-direction." *Journal of Consulting and Clinical Psychology* (1968), *32* (1), 35–41.

Homme, L. E., P. C. De Baca, J. V. Devine, R. Steinhorst and E. J. Rickert. "Use of the Premack Principle in controlling the behavior of nursery school children." *Journal of the Experimental Analysis of Behavior* (1963), *6,* 544.

Kennedy, A. and C. Wilcutt. "Praise and blame as incentives." *Psychological Bulletin* (1964), *62,* 323–32.

Lefcourt, H. M., L. Lewis and I. W. Silverman. "Internal vs. external control of reinforcement and attention in a decision-making task." *Journal of Personality* (1968), *36* (4), 663–81.

Lipe, D. and S. M. Jung. "Manipulating incentives to enhance school learning." *Review of Educational Research* (1972), *41* (4), 249–80.

Lovitt, C. and A. Curtiss. "Academic response rate as a function of teacher and self-imposed contingencies." *Journal of Applied Behavior Analysis* (1969), (2), 49–53.

Masters, J. C. "Social comparison, self-reinforcement and the value of a reinforcer." *Child Development* (1969), *40* (4), 1027–38.

Packard, R. G. "The control of classroom attention: A group contingency for complex behavior." *Journal of Applied Behavior Analysis* (1970), *3,* 1–4.

Samples, R. E. "Toward the intrinsic." *The American Biology Teacher* (1970), *32* (3), 143–48.

Skinner, B. F. "Beyond freedom and dignity." *Psychology Today* (1971), *5,* 37–80.

Staats, A. W. *Child learning, intelligence and personality: Principles of a behavioral interaction approach.* New York: Harper and Row, 1971.

Winter, S. K., J. C. Griffith and D. A. Kolb. "Capacity of self-direction. *Journal of Consulting and Clinical Psychology* (1968), *32,,* 35–41.

Section 3

Postscripts to Behavior Modification in the Classroom

10

Individualization and Structure in the Classroom

By now many readers must have asked themselves, "What good will it do to increase the motivation of these children when the curriculum material is still inappropriate for them?" The answer is that if you don't individualize the curriculum, and make it more appropriate, you only improve the likelihood of many children suffering increasing frustration and failure. Behavior modification is often used because the child has so often failed, he is no longer motivated to try. Once he is motivated to try again by behavior modification techniques, we must be sure that he can succeed. Rather than the typical regular classroom where it is common for all the pupils to be doing the same task at the same time, the regular class teacher who applies behavior modification *must* in some, if not all cases, individualize instruction. This may mean that his classroom takes on the atmosphere of the old-time one-room school, but that was often an exciting and productive place to learn.

Most books on behavior modification in the classroom have a section or at least a chapter devoted to the new technological advances or to programmed instruction. In one respect we can view technological learning as behavior modification without the human manager. Certainly this seems to provide us with a solution in terms of reducing manpower in the classroom, freeing the teacher for more important tasks and thus circumventing a need for economical aid. However, two problems emerge. One is that of paying for fancy technological gadgets when one of our primary dilemmas is lack of funds. The more sophisticated the teaching machines, the more they are bound to cost. Secondly, the same way that many people detest behavior modification for philosophical reasons, many abhor technological independent learning for the same kinds of philosophical reasons. We know of one educator who breaks into a cold sweat when reading literature concerning teaching machines because she envisions that in the year 2000, the word "teacher" will not be thought of as a person or even an ogre, but as a robot on batteries which hands out potato chips for every right answer recorded on its tape. While this may be an extreme way of thinking, it is not so far-out that it is impossible.

Another new trend is programmed learning. Reading and mathematics educators, desperate for learning results, have convinced school boards to sink considerable funds into programmed materials. Unfriendly views of programmed learning stem from the same two sources as unfavorable views of technological learning—economical and philosophical. It seems then that we have a need for increased manpower, but at a lower cost and in a more personal way. This section contains suggestions for analyzing the course curriculum to make possible selection of self-instructional materials essential to the system.

Individualizing instruction means much more than simply providing a different book in a series for each pupil. There may be group projects with each child working at his particular skill level. Subgroups of children may be able to work together, while others may work individually or be taught by peer or teacher aid. The author recommends that for the more immature child, certain subjects, particularly reading, be broken into at least two or three short lessons a day, using a variety of materials to teach the various skills. The teacher may intersperse these lessons with other academic activities or he may use the time for providing immediate reinforcements such as free-time activities, hobbies or crafts. In contrast, the mature child may prefer sustained academic tasks.

Most behavior problem children are academically retarded (Glavin and Annesley, 1971; Graubard, 1964; Stone and Riley, 1964). The most recent study found extreme underachievement by approximately fifty percent of the behavior problem children. This deserves special emphasis, since it has been assumed by some persons working with these children that if emotional problems were treated, the learning problem would disappear.

Their data strongly suggests that learning problems do not disappear after treatment unless the learning problem receives primary classroom attention. Let the reader ask himself: if you were frustrated and failing every day in your job or school activities, would you be happy and well adjusted, withdrawn and neurotic, or acting-out and a behavior problem?

For these children who have suffered so much school failure, it is usually necessary that diagnostic teaching methods be used. For an excellent book on this topic, see Stephen's *Directive Teaching of Children with Learning and Behavioral Handicaps.* The teacher cannot rely on the old, tried-and-true methods; these have already failed. He must be more specific than simply placing the child at his performance level in curriculum. The material must also be interesting and at the child's maturity level. As shown in the Appendix, available commercial materials can vary greatly in level of sophistication, while being on the same reading level.

Glavin and Annesley's study (1971) showed that there was greater underachievement in reading than in arithmetic among underprivileged, behavior-problem children. Since it is improbable that these children's home environments provide enriched reading opportunities, it is imperative that the educational program for the disturbed child stress reading. Whether reading failure is the cause of the child's behavior problem or not is immaterial. If the reading problem continues, then the chances of the child becoming a delinquent or having adult adjustment problems is greatly enhanced.

Many experts suggest that the answer lies in special academic material designed by the child's teacher. The author could not disagree more with this idea, especially concerning the regular class teacher, for several reasons. There are available numerous commercial materials that can be easily modified to meet this need, and most of them are probably superior to what the already harried teacher could produce. In addition, all teachers have many important tasks which could benefit from their additional time, and the task of preparing quality academic material can be a very time consuming operation. Lists of critically evaluated commercial material, which can be modified for remedial purposes, can be very valuable for the teacher (see Appendix).

A number of questions should be asked when preparing each child's individualized program. What are the terminal behaviors to be learned? Has the student already partly mastered the terminal skill? If so, can commercial material be modified to satisfy only the gaps in his deficiency so that the skill can be learned most economically? If answers can be found to the above questions, the teacher will have a "headstart" in individualizing the child's program.

The preparation of each child's curriculum materials should be broken down into these steps: The teacher should identify and describe the objectives in terms of the terminal behaviors expected of the student. This statement should be as specific and objective as possible so that the teacher can accurately evaluate the student's daily progress and prepare diagnostic test items which are correlated with the specific instruction material. The teacher should break down the objectives into daily tasks to insure a logical and consistent flow of the instructional sequence. The daily tasks should include a number of varied activities with their lengths depending upon the student's attending ability. Varied materials should be collected for the daily tasks (e.g., workbooks, audio visual or programmed materials, textbooks or even library books). It is important that the materials be highly correlated with the terminal objectives of the pupil, and that they be analyzed and assigned to the daily task objectives. For further information on this subject, Mager's *Preparing Instructional Objectives* is recommended.

The classroom teacher should always keep in mind that his role is that of a facilitator for learning rather than the headline actor constantly in the spotlight. His role is somewhat akin to that of a business manager or engineer. He sets up the individualized curriculum directed towards developing a nonsatiating learning program. He programs for challenge, progress and variety in the daily learning tasks. He initiates and maintains movement of the individuals and groups in the classroom tasks. In short, he sees that everything runs smoothly towards the terminal goals set for or by the student.

Aside from Rhodes' classic discussion (1963), scant attention has been given to the curriculum needs of behavior problem children. The Appendix presents a summary and listing of materials ordered and utilized in a research project during the 1968—69 school year (Dowdell and Glavin). Listings have been made separately in the areas of reading, aritbmetic and spelling. Because of the topic of the researcb (resource rooms) and use of reinforcers it was necessary to use academic materials thought more suitable to the unique demands of a resource room.

Structuring the Classroom

The concept of structure set off a great controversy in the field of behavior disordered children when Haring and Phillips (1962) published their research in *Educating Emotionally Disturbed Children*. The authors outlined an overall educational plan for hyperactive and withdrawn children built around the hypothesis that children need order and structure in their classroom. They reported significant achievement gains made by pupils taught with a structured technique in contrast to a permissive one. Berkowitz and Rothman (1960) championed a permissive and highly elastic educational program although they failed to report any data. Since then, Haring and Phillips' research has incurred serious criticism, yet the concept of structure has gained in acceptance while the more traditional and medically oriented permissive approach was being supplanted.

By structure Haring and Phillips were referring to the relationship between behavior and its consequences. The specifics of their philosophy led to a set of procedures which will be elaborated upon at the end of this section in terms of concrete suggestions for the teacher. The main emphasis they propounded, which led to the shift in educational policy, was stressing reasonable effort and achievement. Since then, the idea of what encompasses a structured class has become both enlarged and more ambiguous. This author shall include an emphasis upon the physical environment of the classroom as well as suggestions to teachers for setting the classroom atmosphere.

Recently, O'Leary, Becker, Evans and Saudargas (1969) reported a study which cast doubt upon the importance of a structured classroom. Seven pupils in a second-grade class of twenty-one children were observed concerning their disruptive behavior. Rules, educational structure, and praising appropriate behavior were introduced successively. The effects of rules were not particularly significant. The behavior of most children was not affected by having the afternoon divided into four structured lessons. When a token program was introduced in combination with the above elements, significant results were obtained. This author believes that the results of this study were inconclusive regarding the importance of structure, since the authors introduced single elements of what amounts to the concept of structure, whereas a structured classroom combines many of these elements at one time. Regardless, the importance of the concept of structure in working with behavior-problem students cannot be overlooked.

Physical Environment of the Classroom

The importance of the layout of the classroom should be considered from several vantage points. If a teacher is employing a contract system, it may be that the students are working on several different subjects at tbe same time, which might normally cause interference due to noise, distraction or other factors unless the room is divided into activity areas. (This need not mean a literal division even by such things as screens.) The same need for a division of the room is felt if the teacher uses free-activities as a reinforcement, either in a token system or as an aid in minimizing behavior problems during transititions between subjects for those students who have completed their entire assignment successfully.

The room might be considered in terms of low- and high-strength areas (Haring and Kunzelmann, 1966). These terms refer to the amount of physical movement, verbal communication, noise and other factors which distinguish activities from one another. For example, academic skill learning involving independent seat-work or the various language and communication activities are considered low-strength and placed in two nearby sections of the room, albeit these areas normally would use at least two-thirds of the rooms. Examples of high-strength activities are science, arts and crafts, and social or planning centers which might be placed in opposite corners in the back of the room. The important points are that the areas do not interfere with one another and that each area is arranged for independent use by the children. All material necessary for the activities in that particular area should be available there.

Perhaps the most famous example of classroom layout is Hewett's (1968) engineered classroom which is described in his book, *The Emotionally Disturbed Child in the Classroom.* His classroom is arranged into order, mastery, and exploratory centers to help the child acquire the skills considered desirable. The order center helps the child to attend, respond, and order his behavior by using such activities as puzzles, blocks, etc. The exploratory center invites intellectual curosity and encourages social behaviors with activities related to science, art, and communication. The mastery center focuses on academic assignments. It comprises the major portion of the room and is where the teacher's and pupils' desks are located. Also in this area are two isolated study cubicles to be used when a child becomes distracted.

The centers are utilized for intervention purposes when the child is having trouble with his mastery assignment, but before a teacher sends a child to one of the centers he tries other interventions. The study cubicle might first be tried, then the changing of the child's assignment, or the teacher might use positive or negative social reinforcement in dealing with the child's misbehavior. If these fail, the child might be sent to the exploratory center. The next lower step in the intervention hierarchy is for the child to be sent to the order area. If this does not work, the child is taken out of the classroom and given an assignment. Finally, if all else fails, the child may be given a brief time-out or be sent home for the remainder of the day.

Some operant purists have suggested that this hierarchy of interventions, in which a child can earn an equal number of tokens at any of the activity areas, violates contingency principles. However, Hewett points out that many behavior problem children have been turned off by school, and that he is providing a method of desensitization for them. Regardless, when dealing with behavior problem children *en masse*, it is quite a consolation for the teacher to keep all options open until the final solution becomes "up against the wall!"

Classroom Application of Structure

This section is designed to equip the teacher with practical suggestions for coping intelligently and constructively with typical problems. Strategies are briefly presented which focus on troublesome situations frequently arising out of attempts to plan and execute effective instruction, e.g. grouping. Some basic consideration for the teacher's relationship to his students, and for setting formal classroom requirements are considered.

During a teacher's initial contacts with a class, a very important human drama takes place. This interplay may be seen in three acts. In the first act, students observe the behaviors of the teacher and form hypotheses as to just what kind of person, teacher, and disciplinarian he is. This period usually lasts from two days to a week, but it may be longer. Act Two ends the honeymoon period of teaching a class. Now students consciously begin to test their initial assumptions about the teacher and what they can expect from him and from the class, concerning discipline procedures. Act Three is the period of accommodation or final adjustment.

Several practices seem to enhance a teacher's chance of establishing a desirable climate of classroom behavior during the initial phase. For example, the teacher is wise to try to establish a positive set of expectations for the degrees of learning and the pupil behaviors to be attained. At this time it is important to stress the reasons for the class's existence as well as the obligations of the teacher and students in making the class a successful experience.

The teacher should clearly specify the rules and standards which will govern the class and discuss a rationale for them with the students. Later, the teacher may desire to let the students participate in modifying the rules and standards if such action appears to be needed. It is essential that a teacher be firm, frank, fair, and above all, consistent in enforcing rules regarding behavior and performance. One should not threaten and then give in to a child, but rather be prepared to follow through your words with the appropriate action.

The first sessions of the class should be marked by thorough organization which will facilitate the work of the class. Practices such as these reinforce the idea of a businesslike, serious class. A class period can be conceived of as having three segments: the opening phase, the main instructional activity, and the closing phase. These divisions also apply to the discreet learning activities found in the elementary classroom, such as a reading activity.

Some teachers find it useful to involve the students in an activity so that they have needed time for housekeeping chores. Usually the assignment of reading pages is ineffective for such an activity; something more specific is required, such as the following projects which have proven to be useful:

1. A short quiz of five or ten minutes duration (dittoed or written on the board).
2. A statement or question about which the students must write their reactions. Such an item would be related to the work of the class.
3. Have a student either (a) read a subject-related selection of interest to the class or (b) give an oral report.
4. Have a student give a review or summary of the previous day's work.

Inexperienced teachers commonly make several mistakes during the main instructional period of the class. First, they fail to have all the needed materials for a particular learning activity accessible, thus wasting valuable class time and providing students with an opportunity for disruptive interaction. Students become inattentive and may work on other assignments when teachers fail to give directions in an adequate fashion. Using student assistants or monitors for this activity can do much to help teachers overcome such problems. Related to this problem is the failure of many teachers to have students remove all unneeded materials and books from desks.

Transitions, or the breaks which take place between two learning activities, can be another source of problems. Teachers must anticipate the problems which arise at such times, and handle them so as to minimize a loss of time and reduce opportunities for disruptive student behaviors. This includes anticipating the need for books and other supplies.

Finally, some teachers fail to realize the need for "cushions" in the case of certain activities, such as tests and periods of supervised study. Cushions are activities designed to engage the attention of those pupils who finish a particular task earlier than other pupils. For example, he can take from a decorated bucket near the teacher's desk an envelope containing interesting, supplementary assignments to be done in a brief period. These assignments, which can be worth extra-credit points, can be in envelopes color coded to indicate differing levels of difficulty.

Some teachers create problems for themselves by not allowing adequate time to take care of activities such as the proper re-ordering of the room for the next period or activity, the collection and storage of materials and supplies, the review of material covered, or of future assignments previously made, and the orderly dismissal of the class.

When communicating to the students, the teacher should be as concise as possible. Otherwise the children will tend to tune him out. The use of a low, modulated voice tends to increase student attention to directions, and provides a model for the student's interactions, thus supporting a quiet classroom. Oftentimes, when giving either positive or negative reinforcement to a student, the teacher should speak so that only that particular student can hear him. If a student is being disruptive, speaking to him in a low tone prevents him from becoming the center of attention and gaining peer reinforcement. Occasionally, students do not want to be praised in front of their peers for fear of being razzed or thought of as "teacher's pet.". Thus a "positive reinforcement" becomes a negative social reinforcement under certain circumstances and may lead to that student acting-out seconds later to prove to his peers that he is "one of the boys."

The concept of structure implies several procedures for handling the continuously acting-out child who misbehaves or refuses to do his work. If the child is working in a group contingency situation, it is better not to punish the whole group; the teacher may well lose the students' respect or certainly the contingency system will become inoperative. Instead, the child will probably need to be placed on his own contingency program. If the child continues to act out after other interventions have been tried, it is best to remove him from the room to deprive him of his audience and to prevent contagion to his peers. If at all possible, he should be sent to an isolated, nonstimulating room where he can complete his assigned task without distraction, but under observation by an adult. Once the child finishes his task, this serves as his re-entry ticket back to his classroom. He will invariably have regained self-control by this time, and the teacher should be careful not to undo this by scolding or reprimanding him upon his return.

Classroom Atmosphere

There are certain discipline decisions that relate to the climate of the classroom and are intimately affected by the teaching procedures upon which the teacher decides. Each teaching style—whether traditional, contingency contracting, peer tutoring, or self-management—will affect the emotional tone of both student-teacher and student-student relations. If a teacher chooses to combine several styles of teaching at one time, he will need to be careful in making discipline decisions because they *should* vary at any one time, depending upon the type of teaching style being utilized. For a complete analysis of this subject see Mosston's (1972) *Teaching: From Command to Discovery*. If the teacher is injudicious in his discipline decisions, the students are likely to rebel at the teaching style being used and retreat to a more familiar style. One approach to discipline decisions is discussed in the chapter on managing classroom behavior.

Interventions by Using Individualization or Structure

By working on improving the curriculum in a classroom the teacher aids both the disruptive child and prevents others from achieving that dubious title. The same results could be accomplished in maintaining many behavior problem children in the regular classroom if their programs were properly structured. These indirect approaches to intervention or prevention of behavior-disordered children are often overlooked in discussions and in the professional literature, but the regular classroom teacher, by utilizing them, can play a very vital role in aiding children. Both approaches provide ways of assisting the behavior problem child by working indirectly on his problem. When helping the child through his curriculum, the teacher is primarily concerned with such questions as where the material should begin, how it should be introduced, how to adopt it to the child's level and needs, and how fast it should proceed. Structure includes not only the forementioned ways of maintaining a disruptive child in his regular classroom; it includes adjustments within the school such as placement with specific teachers where disruptive children are most likely to make progress, resource rooms, and so forth.

References

Berkowitz, P. H. and E. P. Rothman. *The Disturbed Child: Recognition and Psychoeducational Therapy in the Classroom.* New York: New York University Press, 1960.

Dowdell, E. and J. P. Glavin. "Instructional Material Used in Elementary School Resource Rooms in Reading, Spelling and Arithmetic." Mimeographed. Philadelphia, Pa.: Philadelphia Schools, 1968–69.

Glavin, J. P. and F. R. Annesley. "Reading and Arithmetic Correlates of Conduct-Problem and Withdrawn Children." *The Journal of Special Education* (1971), 5(3).

Graubard, P. "The extent of academic retardation in a residential treatment center." *Journal of Educational Research* (1964), 58, 78–80.

Haring N. G. and E. J. Phillips. *Educating Emotionally Disturbed Children*. New York: McGraw-Hill Book Co., 1962.

Haring, N. G. and H. Kunzelmann. "The Finer Focus of Therapeutic Behavioral Management." Jerome Hellmuth. (ed.), *Educational Therapy*, Vol. 1. Seattle, Wash.: Special Child Publications, Inc., 1966.

O'Leary, K. D., W. C. Becker, M. D. Evans and R. A. Saudargas. "A token reinforcement program in a public school: A replication and systematic analysis." *Journal of Applied Behavior Analysis*, (1969), 2, 3–13.

Rhodes, W. C. "Psychological Techniques and Theory. Applied to Behavior Modification." *Exceptional Children* (1962), 28, 333–38.

Stephens, T. M. *Directive Teaching of Children with Learning and Behavioral Handicaps*. Columbus, Oh.: Charles E. Merrill, Inc., 1970.

Stone, F. B. and V. N. Rowley. "Educational disability in emotionally disturbed children." *Exceptional Children* (1964), 30, 423–26.

11

The Teacher Variable

More educational research focuses on changing student behavior than on changing teacher behavior. This is probably not unnatural, since many people, including teachers, prefer that "someone else" be the subject of an experiment. Undoubtedly, the majority of teachers are more comfortable with strategies such as behavior modification and group counseling designed to modify student behavior, than they are with having similar strategies applied to themselves as teachers.

But as Rasof (1966) points out, the teacher is responsible for the successes and failures of the students, and they in turn are responsible for the successes and failures of the teacher. Students are not the only manipulatives present in the classroom. The relationship is ecological. And similarly, as teachers believe they can shape and manipulate student behavior, so can a feedback device, an observer, a supervisor, or the classroom setting itself shape teacher behavior and attitudes. Recent research, while not voluminous, does suggest ways that a teacher's attitudes and behavior can be and are affected in his teaching. Pre- and in-service training and variables operating upon the teacher in the classroom are important aspects in the shaping of more effective teaching behaviors.

Pre-and In-service Teacher Training

Recognizing that teacher behavior and attitudes have much to do with the achievement of students, researchers have made efforts to identify and correlate teacher behaviors according to their demonstrated effects on pupils, a concept generally termed "teacher effectiveness." Two ways that this identification and change have been operationally attempted in pre-service and in-service teacher training involve behavior modification and modeling.

Behavior Modification and Teacher Training

There are few studies in teacher training regarding the use of behavior modification. Those that do exist, generally provide laboratory-like settings, such as microteaching, to control as many variables as possible. Kelly (1971) utilized what he called behavior modification, to increase the interviewing skills of counselor trainees. One group of trainees received self-reinforcement by viewing videotapes of their interviews. A second group of trainees received videotape self-reinforcement, but in addition received positive verbal feedback from the trainer. These two groups did not differ significantly in learning the interviewing skills, although both groups did better than a control group, which received neither form of feedback. The subjects felt that the clear explanations of the specific behaviors to be learned, provided by the trainer, were a most valuable learning device.

In a study conducted to increase counselor's verbal empathy rates with their clients, baseline empathy rates were established for each trainee (Carlson, 1970). Subsequently, verbal reinforcement was given the trainee for verbal empathy responses which exceeded his baseline rate. A second group of trainees received feedback in the form of response charts but received no verbal reinforcement from the trainer. The group receiving the reinforcement performed better than the group receiving feedback alone, but the results were not significant. Although two studies can hardly be termed conclusive, both do suggest that feedback alone provided to the trainee may influence his teaching behavior, just as much as feedback plus social reinforcement.

Modeling, Feedback and Teacher Training

An operational method considered to be effective in changing teachers' behaviors in training, is interaction analysis. Research demonstrates that the feedback a teacher receives from the interaction analysis scale itself is made more effective when used in conjunction with counseling from a teacher supervisor. Also, the most effective use of the instrument includes self-reinforcement from interaction analysis, video-tapes of the teacher, and verbal approval from a teaching consultant. Another important element in the use of interaction analysis is the effect of modeling, the demonstration of preferred teaching behaviors that the scale provides. This is especially effective with inexperienced teachers who have not developed a classroom repertoire of teaching behaviors.

Kidd (1971) significantly increased the rate at which teachers reinforced student behaviors by using modeling and feedback. Use of videotape playbacks of teacher performance additionally increased the teacher rate of reinforcement. A study of the effects of modeling and feedback on attending and responding behaviors of behavior problem boys found that the boys' motivation increased as their attending and responding behaviors increased. However, when they were returned to their regular classrooms, the new behaviors regressed. According to the experimenter, this happened because the boys were given very little opportunity to exhibit their new behaviors in their regular classrooms, and the teacher behavior in regular classrooms did not fit the student changes effected. (Glass 1971).

Teacher Behavior as Affected in the Classroom

Factors determining the effectiveness of the teacher in the classroom setting include a dissimilarity of values between the teacher and the students, the teacher's perception of his role, the internality-externality of the teacher compared to that of his students, teacher expectations as they affect his performance and attitude, the teacher's residual prejudices, the reinforcements he receives in terms of behavior modification, and the achievement and attitudes of the students. All these factors can and do influence teacher effectiveness and behavior. But as sure as these disparities exist within the teacher, there may be ways that the teacher can engineer the classroom and his own attitudes to allow for and even take advantage of these disparities.

As self-concept is critical to student achievement, so is self-concept central to teacher effectiveness (Norris 1971; Vonk 1971; Barck 1969).

Accordingly, a fundamental problem with which teachers must deal is the maintenance of their self-concepts, which are in large part determined by student achievement and attitudes toward the teacher. Thus, if a teacher has low expectations and places low value upon the students, he will in turn receive negative feedback from the students. This will lower his self-esteem as he is lowering his student's self-esteem.

The phenomenon of the idealistic teacher, fresh from college, who is unable to cope with the realities of the classroom and eventually resigns himself to a monitor's role within the classroom, is referred to repeatedly throughout the literature of education. For example, Weaver (1970) found that the expectancies of teachers of educable mentally retarded students have a significant effect on the teacher's verbal interaction with these children, an interaction critical to the children's achievement and attitude reinforcement and, at the same time, important to the teacher's feedback and diagnosis system. Passow (1966) noted that teachers of ghetto children experience a substantial decrease in self-concept as they face the achievement and behavior problems of these children. In a study on teacher satisfaction in ghetto secondary schools, it was found that satisfaction was related to the teacher's ideology. The authoritarian teacher who typically dislikes conflict, had difficulty coping with all the conflict and was highly dissatisfied, while the reciprocal teacher thrived on the give and take of conflict (Mann 1971). In response to the hypothesis that special education teachers leave teaching because of the demands on them, Bruno (1971) sought to determine why some teachers could evidently tolerate difficult students while others could not. Those who left special education were more psychologically oriented, more nurturant to their students. Those who remained, however, were more politically and economically oriented and were more social science oriented. If those who are more nuturing are the best teachers, as Day (1971) and Vonk (1971) suggest, special education may be losing its most effective teachers, and those remaining may be primarily economically motivated.

There have been no studies which have determined specifically how much training a teacher needs to implement a token system. Studies such as Kuypers, et al. (1968) have shown that the naive teacher could bring about some behavioral change if she was provided with consulting support. My own experience teaching behavior modification principles to undergraduate and graduate students suggests that the basic procedure is learned very quickly. However, once the students apply the technique in their own classrooms, they tend to be satisfied to remain at the extrinsic reinforcement level much longer than is necessary.

While all but a few students have successfully completed action research projects, it is interesting to note that a few students, who were quite outspoken in class in criticizing behavior modification procedures, managed to misinterpret their own data and claimed their projects had failed. This suggests the strong emotional reaction which is often encountered when behavior modification is discussed with educators. While supervising one student's practicum, her first response was, "I used behavior modification last year, but I don't anymore." After observing her class several times, it was obvious that she demonstrated many excellent teaching qualities: She stated firmly and clearly the consequences of the few severe disturbances in the class; she individualized each child's academic work commensurate to his ability; and she made the classroom rules and routines clear. Although she taught a class of eight acting-out, emotionally disturbed boys, this "natural" teacher experienced few outbursts from the children. Closer examination revealed that she dealt with each child consistently, giving frequent praise for their successes and ignoring or using vicarious reinforcement to handle minor infractions. For example, rather than remind a child that he was slumped in his seat, she strongly praised his neighbor for sitting correctly. The immediate result was much better than if she had used the former method. Yet, because of her strong feelings against behavior modification, she didn't realize that she was expertly applying behavioral principles.

Discussion

The above story has its unfortunate aspect, because all too often the excellent or "natural" teachers have been successfully employing behavioral strategies long before learning theorists such as Thorndike and Skinner announced their clinical findings. Even these teachers, however, had not studied their own behavior with sufficient understanding to be able to formulate exactly what they were doing and what their more unfortunate and ineffectual comrades were not doing. The result is the present state of affairs, where teaching is still considered more of an art than a science, and where each beginning teacher must suffer through the same trial and error learning experience—if they survive it. Hopefully, behavior modification principles will have a much greater impact upon this dilemma in the future than it has at present. Behavior modification has certainly had a tremendous impact on the functioning of the teacher in many American classrooms. The teacher is now free to teach, and the students free to learn in an atmosphere conducive to both. Many teachers have marveled at the accomplishments of the educational process when behavioral techniques were employed. Unfortunately, many educators are still skeptical or seem shocked when first exposed to the idea that there are systematic ways of influencing the behavior of others. Hopefully, this climate is changing and will continue to change. With this in mind, it should be incumbent upon every educator to familiarize himself with the principles of behavior modification for use in the classroom.

The prevailing historical model of focusing on the teacher has led to certain blind spots among educators. It has promoted a way of viewing the classroom as if it were composed of two-person units—the teacher and individual student in interaction. The history of this model has recently been disputed and the effect of a teacher's behavior is now viewed as being mediated by classroom group processes and not as occurring in two-person units. For instance, when a teacher gives the class a direction, responses to it are influenced not only by his relationships with the students as individuals, but also by the feelings, attitudes, and relationships that are shared within the peer group. Every classroom manifests group influence of one sort or another, and whatever the teacher does, the group gets involved in mediating that behavior for its members.

The classroom can be viewed as a meeting ground for the collective peer group, the teacher, the students, and the academic curriculum. Teaching and learning are complementary acts that involve a host of interpersonal processes. When these take place in the classroom it is complicated, and is affected by the relationships among students and between the students and the teacher. In some classrooms, the learning process is enhanced by these relationships that actively support a productive learning atmosphere; in others, it is inhibited. The teacher's instructional style, and the curriculum, the student's feelings about himself and his academic abilities, and the nature of the interpersonal relationships in the classroom are all major influences on the teaching-learning process.

References

Barck, P. H. "Teacher attitudes toward self appraisal." Doctoral dissertation, University of Arizona, *Dissertation Abstracts International* (1969), *30* (5).

Bruno, F. B. "Life values, manifest needs and vocational interests as factors influencing professional career satisfaction among teachers of emotionally disturbed children." Doctoral dissertation, Wayne State University, *Dissertation Abstracts International* (1971), *31* (8).

Carlson, K. W. "Reinforcement of empathy: An operant paradigm for the training of counselors." Doctoral dissertation, Northern Illinois University, *Dissertation Abstracts International* (1971), *32* (1).

Day, M. S. "Affective and cognitive goal and behavior in mental retardates." Doctoral dissertation, University of California at Los Angeles, *Dissertation Abstracts International* (1971), *32* (1).

Glass, R. M. "A study of the effects of models and feedback on selected attending and responding behaviors of boys with behavior problems." Doctoral dissertation, Syracuse University, *Dissertation Abstracts International* (1971), *32* (1).

Kelley, J. D. "Reinforcement and acquisition of counseling interviewing skills." Doctoral dissertation, Indiana University, *Dissertation Abstracts International* (1971), *31* (11).

Kidd, J. E. "The influence of selected variables on the reinforcement rates of educators enrolled in a three-week workshop on behavior modification." Doctoral dissertation, University of Virginia, *Dissertation Abstracts International* (1971), *31* (9).

Kuypers, D. S., W. C. Becker and K. D. O'Leary. "How to make a token system fail." *Exceptional Children* (1968), *35* (2), 101-9.

Mann, J. B. "Dimensions of teacher ideology and their relationship to aspects of perceived work environment and job satisfaction in crisis secondary schools." Doctoral dissertation, University of Michigan, *Dissertation Abstracts International* (1971), *31* (8).

Norris, B. E. "A study of self concept of secondary biology teachers and relationship to student achievement and other teacher characteristics." Doctoral dissertation, Ball State University, *Dissertation Abstracts International* (1971), *31* (9).

Passow, A. H. "Diminishing teacher prejudice." In R. D. Strom (ed.), *The inner city classroom: Teacher behaviors*. Columbus, Ohio: Charles E. Merrill, 1966.

Rasof, E. I. and P. R. Hunt. "Discipline: Function or task?" In R. D. Strom (ed.), *The Inner City Classroom: Teacher Behaviors*. Columbus, Ohio: Charles E. Merrill, 1966.

Vonk, H. G. "The relationship of teacher effectiveness to perception of self and teaching purpose." Doctoral dissertation, University of Florida, *Dissertation Abstracts International* (1971), *31* (11).

Weaver, P. A. "Effects of a computer assisted teacher training system and teacher expectancies on teacher-pupil verbal interaction with EMR children." Doctoral dissertation, University of Michigan, *Dissertation Abstracts International* (1970), *30* (2).

Appendix: Evaluation of Commercial Curriculum Materials

The following is a summary and listing of materials ordered and utilized in a Resource Room project during the school year 1968–69. Listings have been made separately in the areas of reading, phonics and arithmetic, and spelling.

Instructional Material for Reading

The following materials are suggested as core materials to be used in Resource Rooms for teaching the basic reading program. The teacher should check to see that the series chosen has not been used with the child at some previous time.

New Skilltext, Charles E. Merrill Books, Inc., 1300 Alum Creek Drive, Columbus, Ohio, 43216.
    This is a good developmental program providing practice exercises in work text form that can be adapted to use in fifteen-minute time segments. Books are available for first to sixth grade. First-grade book can be used to start nonreaders in beginning reading if you progress slowly. Teacher-made worksheets are avail-

able for use with the first book. The materials are consumable. It is recommended that consumable books be used in the first and second grades. Teacher's editions are available.

Title	Reading level
Book 1 *Bibs*	grade 1
Book 2 *Nicky*	grade 2
Book 3 *Uncle Funny Bunny*	grade 3
Book 4 *Uncle Ben*	grade 4
Book 5 *Tom Trot*	grade 5
Book 6 *Pat the Pilot*	grade 6

New Practice Reader, Webster Division of McGraw-Hill Book Co., Manchester Road, Manchester, Mo., 63011.

This is a good program for grade levels 2–8, and provides graded reading and practice exercises to accompany each story. It also provides consistent practice in comprehension and work-attack skills, but is somewhat harder than the *New Skilltext* series published by Merrill. We have found this can be used as follow-up to the *New Skilltext* series if the child has completed a book and is not ready to progress to the next level. It also provides material above the sixth grade level if this is necessary. Answer keys and teachers manuals are available.

Title	Reading level
Book A	grade 2
Book B	grade 3
Book C	grade 4
Book D	grade 5
Book E	grade 6
Book F	grade 7
Book G	grade 8

Sullivan Associates Programmed Reading, Webster Division of McGraw-Hill Book Company, Manchester Road, Manchester, Mo., 63011.

These are programmed textbooks with a linguistic approach, from prereading through grade 5, with supplemental story books, word cards, spirit masters and filmstrips, as well as teachers' guides and reading tests. We found these books to be appropriate as adjunct material but did not find them usable as independent material at the earliest levels. The previously mentioned texts are more suitable as core material due to the attention given to reading comprehension skills and inferential thinking ability. See publishers brochure for detailed information on prices and materials available.

Title	Reading level
The Prereader	grade 1
Series 1 Book 1–7	grade 1
Series 2 Book 8–14	grade 2
Series 3 Book 15–21	grade 3

Appendix

Reader's Digest New Reading Skill Builder, Educational Division of Reader's Digest Services, Inc., Pleasantville, N.Y., 10570.

Reader's Digest provides high interest, low vocabulary, supplementary readers designed with accompanying exercises developing comprehension and interpretation. The books are a bit hard for the level at which use is recommended but they are well designed to be broken up into fifteen-minute work periods. Use as an alternative series is recommended if pupil has been exposed to the *New Skilltext* and *New Practice Reader*, or as supplementary material after use in one of those series if a child is not ready to progress to the next level. Detailed information on the books available may be obtained from the publisher's brochure. Teacher's manuals are available.

Title	Reading level
Level 1–1 [1] Part A and Part B	grade 1
Level 2–6 Part A and Part B	grade 2–6

The Reader's Digest series and the materials listed next are high interest, low reading-level books which are suggested to be used for greater motivation, as supplementary books, or wherever the reading level of the book most closely approximates the level on which the child is reading. The first three series mentioned are more highly recommended because of the added advantage of having accompanying practice material for some books in the series.

The Jim Forrest Readers, Harr Wagner Publishing Co., Field Educational Publications, Inc., 609 Mission St., San Francisco, Calif., 94105.

These books provide stories of interest to upper grade children, with the same characters throughout the series and intriguing plots in each book. A teacher's manual is included for the series, and workbooks are available for those books marked with an asterisk.

Title	Reading level
*Jim Forrest and Ranger Don	grade 1.7
*Jim Forrest and the Trapper	grade 1.7
*Jim Forrest and the Ghost Town	grade 1.8
*Jim Forrest and the Bandits	grade 1.9
Jim Forrest and Lightning	grade 1.9
Jim Forrest and Phantom Grater	grade 2.0
Jim Forrest and the Mystery Hunter	grade 2.2
Jim Forrest and the Plane Crash	grade 2.4
Jim Forrest and Dead Man's Peak	grade 2.6
Jim Forrest and the Flood	grade 2.8
Jim Forrest and Lone Wolf Gulch	grade 3.1
Jim Forrest and Woodman's Ridge	grade 3.2

Cowboy Sam Series, Benefic Press, 10300 W. Roosevelt Rd., Westchester, Ill., 60153.

These are high interest, amusing stories about a cowboy and his ranch hands, written on a low reading-level. Three levels of difficulty for each reading level offer flexibility in meeting individual needs. A teacher's manual is available for the series, and workbooks may be obtained to accompany those books marked with an asterisk.

Title	Reading level	Interest Level
Cowboy Sam and Big Bill	preprimary	pp–2
Cowboy Sam and Freckles	preprimary	pp–2
Cowboy Sam and Dandy	preprimary	pp–2
Cowboy Sam and Miss Lily	primary	p–3
*Cowboy Sam and Porky	primary	p–3
Cowboy Sam	primary	p–3
Cowboy Sam and Flop	grade 1	1–4
*Cowboy Sam and Shorty	grade 1	1–4
Cowboy Sam and Freddy	grade 1	1–4
Cowboy Sam and Sally	grade 2	2–5
*Cowboy Sam and the Fair	grade 2	2–5
Cowboy Sam and the Rodeo	grade 2	2–5
Cowboy Sam and the Airplane	grade 3	3–6
*Cowboy Sam and the Indians	grade 3	3–6
Cowboy Sam and the Rustlers	grade 3	3–6

Sailor Jack Readers, Benefic Press, 10300 W. Roosevelt Rd. Westchester, Ill., 60153.

The Sailor Jack Readers provide books which we found to be extremely motivating to children in the Resource Room program. The books provide high interest, low reading-level material at the very easiest levels. While no published workbooks are provided, teacher-made worksheets are available for the books marked with an asterisk. A teacher's guide is provided.

Title	Reading level	Interest level
Sailor Jack and Homer Pots	preprimary	pp–2
Sailor Jack and Eddy	preprimary	pp–2
*Sailor Jack	preprimary	pp–2
*Sailor Jack and Bluebell's Dive	primary	p–3
*Sailor Jack and Bluebell	primary	p–3
*Sailor Jack and the Jet Plane	primary	p–3
*Sailor Jack and the Ball Game	grade 1	1–4
Sailor Jack's New Friend	grade 1	1–4
*Sailor Jack and the Target Ship	grade 2	2–5
*Sailor Jack Goes North	grade 3	3–6

Dan Frontier Series, Benefic Press, 10300 W. Roosevelt Road, Westchester, Ill., 60153.

Exciting adventures hold the reader's attention in these high interest, low reading-level books. We have used these books successfully with some Resource Room pupils. A teacher's manual is available.

Appendix

Title	Reading level	Interest level
Dan Frontier	preprimary	pp–2
Dan Frontier and the New House	preprimary	pp–2
Dan Frontier and the Big Cat	primary	p–3
Dan Frontier Goes Hunting	primary	p–3
Dan Frontier, Trapper	grade 1	1–4
Dan Frontier and the Indians	grade 1	1–4
Dan Frontier and the Wagon Train	grade 2	2–5
Dan Frontier Scouts With the Army	grade 2	2–5
Dan Frontier, Sheriff	grade 3	3–6
Dan Frontier Goes Exploring	grade 3	3–6
Dan Frontier Goes to Congress	grade 4	4–7

Space Age Books, Benefic Press, 10300 W. Roosevelt Road, Westchester, Ill., 60153.

Books in this series are highly appealing to Resource Room pupils, though they do not start on as low a reading-level as the books in the previously mentioned high interest series.

Title	Reading level	Interest level
Peter, The Rocket Sitter	grade 1	1–4
Peter and the Rocket Fishing Trip	grade 1	1–4
Peter and the Rocket Team	grade 2	2–5
Peter and the Unlucky Rocket	grade 2	2–5
Peter and the Big Balloon	grade 2	2–5
Peter and the Rocket Ship	grade 3	3–6
Peter and the Two-Hour Moon	grade 3	3–6
Peter and the Moon Trip	grade 3	3–6

The following books have been used in certain Resource Rooms to great advantage.

New Diagnostic Reading Workbook Series, Charles E. Merrill Publishing Co., 1300 Alum Creek Drive, Columbus, Ohio, 43216.

These consumable workbooks for grades 1–6 provide interesting one-page stories followed by developmental exercises in comprehension, word mastery and independent thinking. Exercises provide a variety of activities and are easily adapted for use in ten- or fifteen-minute time segments. Vocabulary introduction is controlled and a word list appears in the back of first- and second-level books. Answer keys are available for each grade.

Title	Reading level
Mother Goose	Readiness
Nip the Bear	grade 1
Red Deer, the Indian Boy	grade 2
Scottie and His Friends	grade 3
Adventure Trails	grade 4

Explaning Today	grade 5
Looking Ahead	grade 6

Gates, Arthur I. and Celeste C. Peardon, *Reading Exercises,* Bureau of Publications, Teachers College, Columbia University, N.Y.

This booklet, written on varying levels, provides short one-page reading exercises adaptable for use in ten or fifteen-minute time blocks with a variety of accompanying questions testing comprehension. They would be useful for supplementary comprehension development for children weak in this area. They would also be adaptable for use in smaller time blocks, if the necessity arose.

The following consumable duplicated supplementary material can be used to provide practice in related reading skills at various levels.

Reading Thinking Skills Preprimer Level 1 and Level 2, The Continental Press, Inc., Elizabethtown, Pa., 17022.

These packets of worksheets may be used independently or with teacher guidance to develop skills of organization, inference, relationship and vocabulary. They are sequential and easily adapted to use in fifteen-minute time blocks. It is recommended that these materials be used when the pupil has reached the stated *independent* level of reading rather than instructional level.

Title	Reading level
Reading Thinking Skills Preprimer	Level 1, preprimary
Reading Thinking Skills Preprimer	Level 2, primary

Reading Thinking Skills First Reader Level 1 and 2, The Continental Press, Inc., Elizabethtown, Pa., 17022.

These sheets are useful at the 1 and 2 level but also can be used at independent rather than instructional reading levels. Skills in making inferences, organization, seeing relationships, and making judgements are stressed through a variety of activities.

Title	Reading level
Reading Thinking Skills	Level 1
Reading Thinking Skills	Level 2

Using Good English Grade 5 Semester 1, The Continental Press, Inc., Elizabethtown, Pa., 17022.

Thirty sheets provide sixty lessons in grammar dealing with punctuation usage, parts of speech, abbreviation and similar items. We found these useful with upper grade children who were weak in these areas.

Title	Reading level
Using Good English	grade 5

Color Charts and Direct Process Masters, The Instructor Color Charts, F. A. Owen Publishing Co., Dansville, N.Y., 14437.

Owen Publishing Co. provides a set of eight color posters with ten related spirit masters to teach color words. These have been extremely useful in teaching beginning readers basic sight words.

Appendix

Title	Reading level
The Instructor Color Chart	grade 1

Jenn Publications Spirit Masters, 1-598, 1-629, B-193, Jenn Publications, 815–25 E. Market St., Louisville, Ky., 40206.

These individual spirit masters review reading of color words combined with a coloring activity or cross word puzzle, and are suitable for use when color words have been learned.

Title	Reading level
Jenn Publications Spirit Masters (1-598, 1-629, B-198)	preprimary

Instructional Material for Phonics

Both consumable ditto work sheets and consumable phonics books have been utilized in the teaching of phonics at most levels. It is recommended that workbooks be used on a consumable basis for children in grades 1 and 2, and on a nonconsumable basis thereafter.

Phonics We Use, Lyons and Carnahan, Inc., 407 East 25th Street, Chicago, Ill., 60616.

These books, provided on six levels, have been very useful in implementing the phonics program. They are sequential in nature, though additional material was found to be necessary in developing mastery of initial and final consonants, blends and vowels. Teacher's editions are available at each level.

Title	Reading level
Phonics We Use Book A	Preprimary–Primary
Phonics We Use Book B	grade 1
Phonics We Use Book C	grade 2
Phonics We Use Book D	grade 3
Phonics We Use Book E	grade 4
Phonics We Use Book F	grade 5
Phonics We Use Book G	grade 6

Phonics is Fun, Modern Curriculum Press, A subsidiary of Reardon, Baer and Co., 13900 Prospect Rd. Cleveland, Ohio, 44136.

This is an excellent beginning phonics program which gives a variety of practice exercises teaching initial and final consonants and short and long vowels. It is combined with a beginning reading approach which provides three preprimers that are coordinated with the phonics workbook and is very useful with beginning readers who have difficulty learning sight words. It can also be used with the Stern *Structural Reading Program* and the Merrill *Linguistic Readers.*

Title	Reading level
Phonics if Fun Book 1 (a text workbook)	grade 1
Phonics is Fun Book 2	grade 2
Phonics is Fun Book 3	grade 3

Teacher's Manual and Answer Key	grades 1–3
A Big, Big Man	preprimary 1
In the Tent	preprimary 2
A Mule On A Kite	preprimary 3
Phonics Workbook, Book A.	grade 1
Phonics Workbook, Book B.	grade 2
Phonics Workbook, Book C.	grade 3

Beginning Sounds Level 1, The Continental Press, Inc., Elizabethtown, Pa., 17022.
    These twenty-four spirit masters teach nine initial consonants, devoting at least two full pages to each consonant. They are valuable for use at the earliest levels of phonics work.

Title	*Reading level*
Beginning Sounds Level 1	preprimary or grade 1

Beginning Sounds Level 2, The Continental Press, Inc., Elizabethtown, Pa., 17022.
    Sounds taught at Level 1 are reviewed and eight new sounds are introduced, though not at such a slow and thorough rate. Often two consonants are presented on the same page and there is not as much review, though the packet is still useful for review and introduction of the new sounds.

Title	*Reading level*
Beginning Sounds Level 2	preprimary or grade 1

Phonics and Word Analysis Skills, Grade 1 (Part 1), The Continental Press, Inc., Elizabethtown, Pa., 17022.
    This set of thirty spirit masters provides another approach to initial consonants as well as introducing eleven initial consonant blends and four consonant digraphs. Work on the consonant blends and four digraphs is meager and would have to be supplemented with additional materials.

Title	*Reading level*
Phonics and Word Analysis Skills	grade 1

Phonics and Word Analysis Skills, Grade 2 (Part 1), The Continental Press, Inc., Elizabethtown, Pa., 17022.
    This set of thirty spirit masters reviews initial and final consonants, digraphs, and blends, as well as vowels and adding endings. There is insufficient practice provided to utilize this as the main means of teaching these skills but the material is useful for review.

Title	*Reading level*
Phonics and Word Analysis Skills	grade 2

Jenn Publications Spirit Masters, Jenn Publications, 815–25 E. Market Street, Louisville, Ky., 40206.
    Ten spirit masters review twenty initial consonants through coloring and letter

completion exercises. Two consonants are presented on each page, making the sheets more useful for review than for introductory exposure.

Title	Reading level
Jenn Spirit Masters 1-552 to 1-561	grade 1

The following spirit masters deal with a review of final consonants and completion of initial and final consonants in the same word. They should be used in conjunction with a sequential phonics book as these things are introduced.

Title	Reading level
Jenn Spirit Masters B-36 to B-54	grade 2

Jenn Publications provides eleven spirit masters dealing with initial consonant digraphs and initial and final consonant blends, including a test at the end. These sheets are appropriate for use at the second grade level, or when mastery of these skills becomes necessary in the reading program of the pupil.

Title	Reading level
Jenn Spirit Masters B-55 to B-65	grade 2

These 26 vowel sheets teach all the long and short vowels (including *y* used as a vowel) through coloring and writing activities. They are easier than the Continental Press *Vowel Sheets* and should be used prior to them or alternately with them.

Title	Reading level
Jenn Spirit Masters B-68 to B-90	grade 2
Jenn Spirit Masters B-96 to B-98	

Long and Short Vowels, The Continental Press, Inc., Elizabethtown, Pa., 17022.

This series of spirit masters teaches the five long and short vowel sounds of *a, e, i, o,* and *u* plus the additional sounds of double *o* and *ea*. Tests are included at the end. We found these sheets to be more difficult than the Jenn vowel sheets and suggest they be used after that material.

Title	Reading level
Long and Short Vowels	grades 1, 2

Instructional Material for Spelling

In one resource room a number of children received instruction in spelling. The book cited below was found to be extremely useful in this area and is recommended for teaching spelling at any of the levels indicated. Teacher's editions are provided. Many of these materials as well as those that follow in Mathematics which are available from The Continental Press, Inc., may be previewed by the teacher, using the full six-box, elementary-grade catalogue of miniatures provided by the company. If new material is to be ordered this should be done well in advance of the time it will be needed, as it often takes four to six weeks for delivery.

My Word Book, Lyons and Carnahan, 407 E. 25th Street, Chicago, Ill., 60616.

Title	Reading level
My Word Book 1	grade 1
My Word Book 2	grade 2
My Word Book 3	grade 3
My Word Book 4	grade 4
My Word Book 5	grade 5
My Word Book 6	grade 6
My Word Book 7	grade 7
My Word Book 8	grade 8

Instructional Material for Mathematics

Mathematics programs in the schools tend to be largely traditional in nature. Because pupils are at many varied levels of achievement, and in some cases weak only in a particular area of their grade level, it is more advantageous to compile a sequential course of study from individual work sheets than to utilize a preplanned text. Materials for grade levels 1 and 6 are also obtainable from these companies.

Number Exercises, Milliken Publishing Co., St. Louis, Mo.

Worksheets in basic operations are provided on a sequential basis. Very little attention is given to word problems on these levels. The sheets can easily be adapted to individual needs and work in ten-or fifteen-minute time blocks.

Title	Reading level
Number Exercises	grade 2^1
Number Exercises	grade 2^2
Arithmetic Exercises	grade 3^1
Arithmetic Exercises	grade 3^2
Arithmetic Exercises	grade 4^2

Building in Numberland, The Continental Press, Inc., Elizabethtown, Pa., 17022.

This series provides sequential practice in the four basic operations and a brief introduction to fractional parts, measurement, money, and Roman numerals. Considerable attention is given to word problems.

Title	Reading level
Building in Numberland	grade 4^1
Building in Numberland	grade 4^2

Using Numbers, The Continental Press, Inc., Elizabethtown, Pa., 17022.

These sheets provide work similar to the fourth grade sheets with greater emphasis on division, money and fractions. Again approximately 30 percent of the sheets are devoted to the solving of word problems.

Appendix

Title	Reading level
Using Numbers	grade 5[1]
Using Numbers	grade 5[2]

Useful Arithmetic Series, The Continental Press, Inc., Elizabethtown, Pa., 17022.

Provision for the teaching of money and the words associated with it has been made with the use of two special packets of material designed for this purpose. It may be necessary to give considerable additional practice in reading money words such as penny, dime, and dollar.

Title	Reading level
U.S. Money Level 2	grades 2–4
U.S. Money Level 3	grades 2–4

Jenn Publications Spirit Masters, Jenn Publications, 815–825 E. Market Street, Louisville, Ky., 40206.

This company makes spirit masters available on a single sheet basis in reading and arithmetic. A separate catalogue is published for first, second, and third grades, and one for intermediate grades. For specific details on the ordering of materials, the catalogues should be consulted.

Practice Exercises in Arithmetic, Curriculum Planning Committee for Arithmetic Instruction in the Elementary School, Philadelphia Public Schools, Philadelphia, Pa.

Arithmetic drill books at various levels with accompanying answer guides were used with a number of children to provide necessary practice in basic arithmetic concepts. They were especially useful because they were graded, sequential, could be made self checking, and were easily adaptable to ten-or fifteen-minute time blocks.

Title	Reading level
Practice Exercises in Arithmetic Book A	grades 2, 3
Practice Exercises in Arithmetic Book B	grades 3, 4
Practice Exercises in Arithmetic Book C	grade 5
Practice Exercises in Arithmetic Book D	grades 5, 6

NAME INDEX

Allen, D.W., 59, 94
Altman, R., 59
Andrews, H., 75
Annesley, F.R., 20, 51, 120, 121
Armstrong, M., 70
Arnold, C.R., 53
Ayllon, T., 33

Baer, D.M., 44, 49
Bandura, A., 36, 58–9, 60, 61, 63, 90, 112
Barck, P.H., 132
Barrish, H.H., 29, 49, 74
Becker, W.C., 23, 41, 49, 68–9, 70, 71, 123, 133
Benson, C., 49
Berkowitz, P.H., 123
Blackham, G.J., 24, 28, 89
Blanchard, E.D., 58
Broden, M.R., 49, 89
Bronfenbrenner, U., 60
Bruno, F.B., 133
Bryen, D., 61–3
Burns, B., 26

Campbell, N., 88
Carlson, K.W., 131
Carnine, D., 23
Catterall, C.D., 80
Chamberlain, P., 89

Chapman, A., 92
Christine, R.D., 94, 103
Christopolos, F., 6, 7
Clarizio, H.F., 36
Clark, C.A., 69–70
Clark, M., 49
Clark, R., 53
Cody, J.J., 27
Coleman, J.S., 75–6
Conderman, L., 49
Curtiss, K.A., 88, 90, 111

Day, M.S., 133
Davis, F.M., 21
DeBaca, P.C., 111–2 Deno, S.L., 33, 94
Devine, J.V., 111–2
Dickinson, D., 71
Douglass, V., 48
Dowdell, E., 122
Drabman, R., 44, 48
Duncan, A.D., 89
Dunlap, A., 53
Dunn, L.M., 6, 51

Evans, G., 76
Evans, M.D., 123

Ferster, C.B., 33
Fesbach, N.D., 59

Flanders, J., 59
Forness, S.R., 46

Ganzer, V.J., 59
Gittleman, M., 59
Glass, R.M., 132
Glavin, J.P., 20, 21, 29, 46, 47, 51, 98, 99, 120, 121, 122
Glasser, W., 110
Goodman, L., 39–41
Graubard, P., 89, 120
Grieger, R., 76
Griffith, J.C., 109, 113

Hall, E., 10
Hall, V., 53, 89
Haring, N.G., 49, 122, 123, 124
Hewett, F.M., 14, 15, 124, 125
Homme, L., 84, 85, 111–112
Hunt, P.R., 130
Hunter, M., 29

Jenkins, J.R., 33, 94
Jones, R.L., 11, 12
Jung, S.M., 108
Junod, R., 50–51

Kennedy, A., 107
Kennedy, B.J., 88
Kennedy, W.A., 25
Keirsey, D.W., 24
Kelly, J.D., 131
Kidd, J.E., 132
Kolb, D.A., 109, 113
Kothera, R., 49
Kounin, J., 64
Kunzelman, H.P., 49, 124
Kuypers, D.S., 41, 90, 133

La Mancusa, K., 48
Lefcourt, H.M., 113
Lewis, L., 113
Lilly, M., 11, 12, 14
Lipe, D., 108
Long, N.J., 20

Lovaas, O.I., 60
Lovitt, T.C., 88, 90, 111

McAllister, L.W., 49
McCandles, B.R., 26
McDonald, F.J., 58, 59
McKenzie, H.S., 49
Mackie, R.P., 11
McMains, M.J., 90
MacMillan, D.L., 6, 7, 12, 13, 46
McQueen, M.M., 54
Madsen, C.H., 53, 58–59
Maer, M.L., 45
Mager, R., 122
Mallick, S.K., 26
Mann, J.B., 133
Masters, J.C., 109
Mayer, A.R., 27
Minde, K., 48
Minuchin, S., 89
Mischel, W., 58
Misklin, M., 21
Mitts, B., 89
Morse, W.C., 20
Mosston, M., 128
Myrick, R.D., 26

Neisworth, J.T., 33, 94
Nemeth, E., 48
Newland, T.E., 17
Newman, R.G., 20
Nolen, P.A., 49
Norris, B.E., 132

O'Leary, K.D., 41, 44, 48, 58, 69, 123, 133
O'Leary, S., 58
O'Neal, P., 46
Oswalt, G., 76

Packard, R.G., 75, 112
Passow, A.H., 133
Pavlow, I., 33
Pendergrass, V., 27
Perloff, B., 112

Name Index

Phillips, E.J., 122, 123
Polsky, H., 50
Premack, D., 111, 112

Quay, H.C., 20, 21, 29, 44, 46, 47, 51

Rasof, E.I., 130
Reese, E., 33
Renz, P., 6, 7
Rhodes, W.C., 122
Rickert, E.J., 111–112
Risley, T.R., 44
Ritter, J., 58
Robins, L.N., 48
Ross, D., 58–59
Ross, S.A., 58–59
Rothman, E.P., 123
Rowley, V.N., 120

Samples, R.E., 108, 111
Sarason, I.G., 59
Saudargas, R.A., 123
Saunders, M., 29, 49, 74
Schmidt, G., 74
Schwieder, M., 77–79
Scull, N., 86–87
Shoup, M.L., 98, 99
Silberman, A., 28, 89
Silberman, I.W., 113
Skinner, B.F., 33, 106, 134

Smith, E.P., 29
Smith, J.M., 29
Sprague, R.L., 54
Staats, A.W., 54, 109–110
Stackowiak, J.G., 49
Steinhorst, R., 111–112
Stephens, T.M., 121
Stone, F.B., 120
Sulzer, B., 27

Talkington, L., 59
Thelen, M.H., 58
Thomas, D.R., 23, 53, 68–69, 70
Thorndike, R., 33, 134

Ulrich, R., 74

Von Harrison, G., 103
Vonk, H.G., 132, 133

Walberg, H.J., 69–70
Walsh, M.E., 72–73
Weaver, P.A., 133
Weiss, G., 48
Werry, J.S., 20, 29, 46, 47, 48, 51
Wilcutt, C., 107
Winter, S.K., 109, 113
Witt, P., 26
Wolf, M.M., 29, 44, 49, 74
Yelon, S.L., 35, 36

SUBJECT INDEX

The Analysis of Human Operant Behavior, 33
An Educational Intervention for Socially Maladjusted Adolescents, 50–1
Baseline data, collecting, 37
Behavior Modification: definitions, 33–4, evaluation, 38; goals, 46–7, 106–8; implementation, 37–9, 44–6, 106–8, 113–4; strategies, 24
Behavior Modification Techniques in a Normal Public School Classroom, 72–3
Classroom structure: atmosphere, 127–8; beginning school year, 125; definition of, 123; during school day, 125–8; evaluating, 123; physical environment, 123–4
Commercial curriculum material, critical evaluation of, 137–47
Consulting Teacher Program at The University of Vermont, 16
Contingency contracting, 83–8, 91; adjusting nonfunctioning contracts, 91; description of, 92–4; initiating, 38; rules for, 84–5; student's role, 88–91; with a group, 75–7; *see also How to Use Contingency Contracting in the Classroom,* 84
Cottage Six, 50
Decreasing the Calling-Out Behavior of a Second-Year Regular Class, 77–9
Desensitization, 36
Directive Teaching of Children with Learning and Behavioral Handicaps, 121
Developing Sound-Chaining into Words in a Five-Year-Old Mongoloid Girl, 61–3
Deviant classroom behavior: aggressive, acting-out, 26; as affected by teaching styles, 19–20; by entire class (!), 29; effeminate, 25–6; school phobia, 25; truancy, 28
Discrimination learning, 35
Dissimulating, by children, 45–6
Educating Emotionally Disturbed Children, 122
The Emotionally Disturbed Child in the Classroom, 124
Exceptional children, 14–15; assisting the regular class teacher, 14; evaluating, 6; implications for general education, 13; integration versus segregation of, 6; labeling problems, 10; multiply-handicapped, 10; political implications of, 7; professional assistance available, 7, 11, 14; social attitudes toward, 10
Extinction, of behavior, 35

Subject Index

Generalization of behavior, 39, 51–2
How to Use Contingency Contracting in the Classroom, 84
Individualizing instruction: approaches, 8, 94–105, 106–18, 119–22; by precision teaching, 9; by programmed instruction, 9, 120; need for, 119–21; new diagnostic methods, 9; teacher preparation for, 8; using commercial material for, 121–2, 137–47
Interaction, between child and his environment, 19
Modeling, 36, 57–64; compared to operant conditioning, 50; effects of, 58–9; factors influencing effects, 59–60; strategy, 61–3
Modification of Child Behavior, 89
Motivation, 106–8, 113–4; extrinsic versus intrinsic, 44–5; procedures, 34–7
Peer group: contingencies, 75–7; reinforcement and pressure, 74–5
Peer tutoring, 94–105; description, 94–5; history of, 98–9; implications of, 102–3; in a behavioral setting, 99–101; procedure, 100–1; roles of participants, 95–7; selection of tutors, 99–100; underlying dynamics, 104; using reinforcement system, 101
Pennsylvania Conference on Educational Programs for Exceptional Children, 15
Preparing Instructional Objectives, 122
Preventing common class problems, 23
Price-Setting as an Incentive in Behavior Modification, 86–7
Professional Instruction Program (PIP) at Norfolk State College, 15
Programmed Environments for the Developmentally Retarded at The University of Kentucky, 16
Punishment, 36–7

Reduction of Interrupting Behavior in First Grade Children, 39–41
Reducing Behavior Problems: An operant Conditioning Guide for Teachers, 23–4
Reinforcement: by peers, 74–5, history of, 36; of incompatible responses, 35; positive, 34; selection of, 37–8; social, 67–81; vicarious, 63–4
Self-management: by response manipulation, 108; cautions against, 112–3; characteristics of self-managed students, 109–10; controversial aspects of, 106–7; effects of, 111; implications of, 113–4
Social reinforcement: by groups, 75–7; by teacher, 73–4, 79–80; development, 67–8; implications of, 80–1; techniques for classroom application, 79–80
Special education: alternatives to, 11; changes needed, 7; funding problems, 11; manpower needs, 11; organizational structure, 12; professional retraining problems, 12; research projects in, 15–7; *see also Pennsylvania Conference on Educational Programs for Exceptional Children*
Student Motivation and Classroom Management: A Behavioristic Approach, 33
Student's role: as evaluator, 90–1; as record-keeper, 80–90; as reinforcement authority, 90–91; as specifier of tasks, 88
Teachers: as social reinforcers, 68–74; behavioral effect on classroom, 132–3; biases against, 134; consulting with, 20; modeling effects of, 132; speaking voice, 29; style, 127–8; training 131–2
Teaching: From Command to Discovery, 128

Tests, standardized, 8

Time-outs, 27–8

Token economies, problems involved, 41–2

Vicarious reinforcement, 63–4

Voice modulation and behavior control, 29

We Do Not Throw Rocks at the Teacher, 48